BENTLEY

3½ & 4¼ LITRE 1933–40

In Detail

Contents

Introduction

There can have been few makes of car which impressed themselves on the minds of the British public as much as the Bentley did. During the 1920s its sporting achievements were on everyone's lips. Then, after the shock of the company going into receivership, there followed a partnership with the one remaining make which might be said to have an even bigger reputation – Rolls-Royce. Although we now know these pre-World War Two cars as Derby Bentleys, after the factory where the two makes were produced, many people at the time, and even now, refer to them as "Rolls-Bentleys". This name, although frowned on by the company, says much about the way in which the cars were regarded. The new Bentley combined an enduring reputation for high-performance with the magic which went with the name of Rolls-Royce. The result, all were agreed, just had to be the best sports car that money could buy.

This book tries to tell the reader everything about Derby Bentleys – how they were developed,

1933 Park Ward 3½ Litre four-door sports saloon (early design with small luggage boot).

their technical specification, what it is like to own one – within a manageable number of pages. It is aimed at potential as well as existing owners, and tries to encapsulate for both the key facts which any enthusiast for these cars would want to know. It also attempts to place the Derby Bentley in context, by examining its competitors and assessing how the Bentley stood up against them. At the same time, though, it tries to get behind the facts to recreate the atmosphere which existed when they were being produced. While no-one will be surprised to read of the care which went into developing and testing every component of both Rolls-Royce and Bentley cars, some may be intrigued to learn of the apparently haphazard way in which crucial decisions were sometimes made.

In understanding the history of the Derby Bentley it is of course essential to bear in mind the wider background of the troubled 1930s. To begin with, when Rolls-Royce set out to buy the Bentley assets from the receiver their business was suffering badly from the effects of the Depression. Not only were car sales plunging but the Air Ministry had made it clear that no orders for aero engines could be expected for some considerable time. Thus the company's main objective was to obtain the goodwill which went with the Bentley name, and then "to use that goodwill in getting more chassis work into Derby". Later on, of course, matters were reversed; the rearmament programme put increasing pressure on aero engine projects, and the resources available for car development were correspondingly reduced. Finally, just when

the finest Derby Bentley of all was being made ready for the 1939 London and Paris Motor Shows, international events intervened and brought all car production to a halt.

Despite these pressures, the Derby Bentleys – 3½ Litre, 4¼ Litre and Mark V – were an outstanding sales success. How much of this can be laid at the door of the Experimental department at Derby, and how much at a different door, specifically in Conduit Street in London's West End, where the Sales department were located, is a subject which could be debated for a long time. Wherever the credit may lie, the company as a whole managed to produce and sell a more expensive car at twice the rate of either of its nearest competitors, and that was no mean achievement. Even more importantly, these sales were gained without apparently making any significant dent in the sales figures of the two Rolls-Royce models – this having been the directors' greatest fear from the start.

It would not be possible, so long after the event, to carry out such a detailed analysis of these happenings if the company records had not been preserved in such depth. Fortunately for us they are kept in impeccable order at Hunt House, home of both the Rolls-Royce Enthusiasts' Club and the Sir Henry Royce Memorial Foundation. I am deeply grateful to the two key individuals involved in these organisations, Peter Baines and Philip Hall, for the enormous help and cooperation they have given me. Equally I want to record my thanks to the Bentley Drivers' Club, and in particularly to

Simon Towle, for similar assistance. Will Fiennes, Derby Bentley expert and restorer supreme, willingly gave up a slice of his valuable time to go over the finer technical details of these cars, which was of inestimable value to me. And finally I want to thank James Fack, who has been of constant assistance to me ever since he learned of this project, and who volunteered to read through the manuscript.

None of this is to imply that these individuals, or any others, take responsibility for what follows; if there are any mistakes, they are mine, and I can only hope that they do not spoil your enjoyment of the book. More importantly, though, I shall take the book to be a success if existing owners of Derby Bentley learn something new from its pages, and if prospective owners are inspired to turn ambition into acquisition.

Nick Walker
Ilmington, May 2002

Above: 1938 Vanden Plas 4¼ Litre four-seater tourer.
Below: *1933-34 3½ Litre Owen sedanca coupé.*

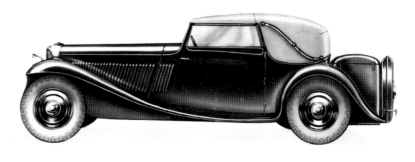

Chapter One

The Bentley Company

If we are to appreciate how the Bentley was perceived in the 1930s, it is important to understand the reverence in which its 1920s predecessor was held. Not only had the marque won the world-famous Le Mans race on five occasions, but the names and exploits of its drivers were familiar to thousands. It would be wrong to say that the "Bentley Boys" were as well known in their day as the Beatles in theirs, but the comparison is not too fanciful, given that there was no television coverage in those far-off days.

More than that, though, there was something particularly British about this car from the north-west suburbs of London. Monsieur Bugatti's supposed remark that "Mr Bentley makes the fastest lorries in the world" only confirmed what the British enthusiast knew already – that the French were a bunch of effete artists, more concerned with appearance than achievement. "Their" Bentley, by contrast, sat high off the ground (as a car should), delivered its power in measured thumps (as a car should) and went like stink (provided it had not been loaded with too heavy a body).

Even the founder, Walter Owen Bentley, was particularly British. He was a gentleman, for a start, coming from a moneyed family and attending a good-class public school (Clifton). Moreover, as befitted a British gentleman, his behaviour was always above reproach. In the way he treated his shop-floor workers, in the uncomplaining way in which he suffered reverses of fortune, in the self-effacing style of his autobiography, he was the

model to which all British men aspired.

From his background one might have expected "WO" to have been steered into one of the professions – medicine, perhaps, or architecture. Clearly the young WO was going to have nothing of that, and in 1904, at the age of sixteen, he began an apprenticeship in railway engineering with the Great Northern Railway at Doncaster. This was a not uncommon route in those days in the engineering industry, even for those who aspired to a managerial position; the belief was that no-one could run a drawing-office or a factory if he had not mastered the manufacturing processes involved. There was less specialisation, too, so that a mechanical engineer was just that, as a training in one branch (such as railway engineering) by no means precluded a move into another.

Such a move was exactly what WO made when he had completed his apprenticeship. He joined the National Motor Cab Company in Hammersmith, West London, having already shown a preference for the internal combustion engine by racing a motorcycle at Brooklands. Soon, however, his desire for greater things – and the existence of some family money – caused him to move on again. In 1912 he and his brother Henry ("HM") took over the British importers of the French DFP car, renaming it Bentley & Bentley. DFP had up to then used proprietary engines, but had just changed to making their own engine.

It could well be that WO, ever the engineer, spotted the potential in the design of this engine. Certainly it was not long before he was carrying

out his own modifications, initially with aluminium-alloy pistons and later with a redesigned camshaft. Since competition was the key to sales success in those days he entered the car at a number of Brooklands events, with great success, and then went on to establish new class records. The DFP company must have been impressed, as in 1914 it adopted aluminium pistons as standard, a very advanced feature for the time.

WO's expertise with engines, and his experience with aluminium pistons in particular, was put to good use during World War One when he served with the Royal Naval Air Service (and later the Royal Air Force). The RNAS Technical Board was responsible for developing French rotary aero engines being made under licence in Britain, which culminated in WO producing two total redesigns. His BR1 and BR2 engines were the first to use an aluminium cylinder block with steel liners. In this way he obtained valuable experience of aeronautical engineering, which at the time was regarded as the most demanding branch of mechanical engineering much as aerospace work is today. It is no coincidence that a number of leaders of the postwar motor industry were involved with aero engines during the war.

The war over, WO returned to Bentley & Bentley and selling DFP cars. However, to judge by the speed with which he had designed his first car, the 3 Litre (it gained two pages' coverage in *The Autocar* in May 1919), he must have been well advanced with his thinking while the war was still going on. Not that such thinking had encompassed such mundane aspects as production and finance; at this May date he still had both to find premises and produce his first car. Such an order of priorities might suggest an ominous warning of what was to come. He managed to show a chassis at the Olympia Show that same year, and he had even formed a separate company to do so. The fact that certain key components of the engine were either missing or dummied in wood was spotted by neither journalists nor the public.

Another laudatory article in *The Autocar* just after the Show (four pages this time) declaimed that "it is the intention of the manufacturers to test the car with more than usual thoroughness ere the first examples are allowed to reach the hands of private owners." Decoded, this meant that the car was still being developed and the factory at Cricklewood had yet to be built. Why it was necessary to build a special factory, financed by a mortgage,

WO Bentley in the very first Bentley, 3 Litre chassis EXP 1, in January 1920.

The most famous radiator badge in England during the 1920s.

A 1923 3 Litre with drophead coupé body by Penman of Dumfries.

The classic Vanden Plas sports tourer body, here on a 1924/5 3 Litre chassis.

rather than rent cheap premises to begin with has never been explained, but it meant that the new company started as it was to go on – perpetually short of cash. And such working capital as there was must have been severely strained by the time taken before any cars reached the public. The first was delivered in September 1921, almost two years after the prototype chassis was shown at Olympia.

Despite the long wait, once deliveries started the car was welcomed on all sides, notwithstanding a price for the "sporting four-seater" of £1295. WO's intentions had been clear from the outset: he wanted to produce a sporting car, so that enthusiastic motorists could buy a British product rather than one from abroad. The way in which the engine was designed – and the engine was always the most important part of a WO Bentley – suggested not only that it would give

sparkling performance but also that it would be reliable in arduous conditions. Although the stroke, at 149mm, was on the long side, this was counter-balanced by a maximum engine speed of only 3500rpm. An overhead camshaft and four valves per cylinder were not uncommon at the time, but such features as (originally) dry-sump lubrication, a five-bearing crankshaft and rigid bolting of the bearing end-caps were more suggestive of racing practice. Indeed, "Sammy" Davis, an aero-engine colleague of WO and later one of the Bentley Boys, commented that the first time he saw the drawings he thought it was "as near a racing car as no matter".

The hopes of the enthusiasts were soon fulfilled with an early win at Brooklands in 1921 in a pre-production car, followed by a resounding team award for three cars in the Tourist Trophy the following year. Very soon, however, it became clear that not all buyers shared the desire for an out-and-out sports car. Whereas the intention had been to produce only open cars, customers quickly began to order saloons from their coachbuilders. This raised two problems: firstly closed bodies were significantly heavier than open ones, and secondly they normally required more space than the 117.5in-wheelbase chassis could provide. Bentley's immediate response, in 1923, was to offer a longer wheelbase (130in) chassis, which became in effect

the standard model from then on. This solved the space problem but left the 3 Litre engine some-what lacking in power for such a large car.

This was the period when large, powerful, expensive cars were synonymous with continental touring. For those who could afford it, speed and cubic capacity were what mattered for this type of motoring, and a form of horsepower race ensued. For WO, who was very familiar with motoring conditions on the continent, a larger capacity engine seemed essential. Thus, the story goes, he was testing an experimental 4¼-litre six-cylinder car in France when he found himself in a race with what turned out to be the prototype Rolls-Royce Phantom I (with a massive 7.7 Litres). Although it transpired that the Bentley was the Rolls's equal in performance, WO decided that even more engine capacity was needed, and out of that experience was born the 6½ Litre model.

The new large model, introduced in 1925, was made available in three different wheelbase sizes, from 132 inches to 150. The longest of these three was the equal of the Phantom I (launched the same year), and was clearly intended for the sort of grand formal coachwork which had never been WO's intention at the beginning. Thus the company's clientele was starting to split in two: those who were sporting enthusiasts pure and simple, and others who liked the idea of the car's sporting

A 1925 3 Litre Weymann saloon by Freestone & Webb.

The start of the 1927 Le Mans race. No 3 (the eventual winner) is the 3 Litre driven by Benjafield and Davis, and No 1 is Clement's 4½ Litre.

image but who were prepared to sacrifice some performance for comfort. The 6½ Litre car catered for the latter group, while the former continued to buy the 3 Litre, usually with open bodies.

In the face of all this apparent success, the company's financial affairs took a surprising turn for the worse. Just which activity tipped the cash-flow the wrong way is impossible to tell; perhaps it was the development cost of the new model, perhaps the increasing expenditure on the racing programme. Whatever the reason, WO initially approached Dr "Benjy" Benjafield, who as well as being a personal friend and one of the Bentley Boys happened to be extremely wealthy. Benjafield agreed to help, provided his involvement remained confidential; not only did he finance the company's racing activities, but for a time he personally owned the works team cars. Even this, though, was not enough, and WO felt it necessary to approach the multi-millionaire (and Bentley Boy) Woolf Barnato for more substantial assistance. There followed in June 1926 a company reconstruction, which left Barnato holding a large majority of both the ordinary and the preference shares, with WO's holding and that of his brother HM very much reduced. HM was severely displeased with the terms Barnato had imposed, and left the company.

Barnato was an unusual individual in many ways. When a person is left a huge fortune (from diamond and gold mining in South Africa) at an early age, the natural assumption is that he is going to develop into a spendthrift with no financial sense. Yet if there is one character trait which all who knew him agree Woolf Barnato possessed, it was business and financial acumen of a high order. Given this, one might ask why he had decided to prop up an ailing business. The answer, as WO himself hinted at years later, was "because if he hadn't there would have been no more nice Bentleys for him to race". Even so, it should be noted, Barnato negotiated some very tight terms before he provided the finance.

This is not to suggest that Barnato was anything other than correct in all his dealings, both with the company and with WO himself. His terms may

have upset WO's brother, but in hindsight they do not look unreasonable given that the alternative would probably have been receivership. At a personal level all the signs were that relations between Barnato and WO were, if not warm, certainly friendly. This was all to the good, for WO now found himself working as managing director (and later joint MD), answerable to a board of which Barnato was the chairman. All the evidence is that, while Barnato had strong views on such matters as finance and model policy, he always deferred to WO in matters of design.

While the spotlight was on the more glamorous 6½ Litre model, the sporting customers were not forgotten. It had become clear that they needed more performance – and even a little more room – than the 3 Litre could offer, so it was for them that the 4½ Litre model was developed. This model's engine required comparatively little design time, since it was effectively two-thirds of a 6½ Litre. In other words it had four cylinders instead of six, but retained the bore and stroke of the larger engine (100 x 140 mm). The standard wheelbase was

again 130 inches, to cater for formal bodywork if required, although some special shorter (117.5in) chassis were constructed.

Now began the most famous period in the history of the Bentley company, when on the face of things they could do nothing wrong. The 1927 Le Mans saw the first of what were to be four successive wins for Bentley, on this occasion by a 3 Litre piloted by "Sammy" Davis and "Benjy" Benjafield. This was the year of the famous White House Corner crash, from which "Old Number One" emerged to take the prize. The incident, which was not of Davis's making, further enhanced the marque's reputation for reliability, with dramatic pictures in the press of the car continuing with alarming damage to its front offside. As Davis wrote afterwards, apart from shoring up the accident damage as quickly as possible "nothing whatever was required for the car. The bonnet was never lifted, all eight plugs were firing at the end, the dynamo charged full, the S.U. carburettor pistons did not stick, the tyres gave no trouble, and the engine was every bit as lively when the old car

Barnato and Rubin, winners of the 1928 Le Mans, with their 4½ Litre.

The best "WO" Bentley of all? A Speed Six chassis.

high maximum speed and their reliability. Hence he was particularly interested in taking part not only in the Le Mans race each year but also in such events as the Brooklands "Double Twelve" – the nearest Brooklands could get to running a 24-hour event without upsetting the local residents.

Brooklands had other attractions. Not only were events there covered in great detail in the British press, but the people who went there were largely drawn from Bentley's target market. The Brooklands slogan was "the right crowd and no crowding"; if these days we find the phrase too snobbish, in the 1920s it summed up attitudes perfectly. These were the people who could afford both to buy expensive cars and, if they wanted, to race them. If they preferred merely to watch, at least they could go home in their heavy, saloon-bodied Bentleys and flatter themselves that they had bought the right car – a superbly made British car with an unbeatable sporting pedigree. Thus Brooklands typified two contradictory market segments, the sporting motorist versus the carriage trade. Increasingly, the company realised it had to have products which appealed to both types of customer.

Meanwhile development and racing continued apace. A team of three 4½ Litre cars carried the flag at the 1928 Le Mans, and one of them won, driven by Barnato and Rubin. Back at the factory, further work on the 6½ Litre engine saw the emergence at the end of that year of the Speed Six version, possibly the best Cricklewood Bentley of all. It boasted a second carburettor and a raised compression ratio, and its arrival clearly satisfied WO, who is thought to have preferred the model above any other of his creations.

The sporting potential of the Speed Six was immediately evident, and an example was entered for Le Mans in 1929, alongside three 4½ Litre models. The outcome was the Bentley company's finest hour: the Speed Six won, driven by Barnato and "Tim" Birkin, and the remaining cars filled the next three places. The news of this overwhelming win went round the world, turning the Bentley name into a household word. Two weeks later came the BARC six-hour race at Brooklands, and a Speed Six won again, this time driven by Barnato and Jack Dunfee. Later that year Clement and Barclay drove a 4½ Litre to win the BRDC 500-mile race, also at Brooklands; the Speed Six came second, although it put up the fastest lap.

No-one has doubted, either at the time or since, that all this feverish activity on the racing front

finished as it was at the commencement".

A pre-production example of the new 4½ Litre had been entered that year, driven by Clement and Callingham, and attracted much publicity by leading the race for a time. Unfortunately it then became involved in the White House Corner incident, leaving the remaining 3 Litre to struggle home for victory. However the new model scored its first victory only two months later, when it won the 24-hour Grand Prix of Paris, this time driven by Clement and Duller. Further wins, particularly at Brooklands, soon followed. The predominance of Le Mans and Brooklands in the Bentley racing programme was no accident, and indeed was carefully calculated by WO in his role as racing manager for the company, a role which Barnato was happy for him to continue alongside his design work. WO sought out those events which would exploit his cars' two greatest features: their helped to sell cars, and it did so to both audiences. The sporting buyers, provided they could afford these expensive cars, hardly had to think about their choice – the results in competition said it all. The "carriage trade" on the other hand, who might otherwise have considered a Rolls-Royce or Daimler, were entranced by the image of power and performance that went with a Bentley. From the beginning WO had been convinced that a racing programme was an essential part of selling his cars, and he must have been right.

The question which no-one has answered satisfactorily is whether the racing programme was affordable. In his autobiography WO quoted figures for the company's annual expenditure on racing which appear laughably small, even when one allows for Benjafield's clandestine help. Perhaps his figures were what actually appeared in the company's management accounts, but it would seem that many of the costs were "buried" under other headings. One cannot but observe that WO's apparent naivety in this matter may have been symptomatic of his wider attitude to financial affairs. (Years later he was still protesting that the company had made a profit in its last 18 months at Cricklewood, as if that rather than cash was the deciding factor.)

It would certainly seem that Barnato did not have a high opinion of WO as a businessman. No doubt for that reason, in 1927 he introduced a banking friend, the Marquis of Casa Maury, as joint managing director alongside WO. One might have expected this to have resulted in much tighter control of costs, but such evidence as there is suggests not. Casa Maury, for a start, seems to have been a disappointment, and was soon demoted. Meanwhile Barnato and the other directors appear to have increasingly been at odds with WO as to the direction in which the company should go. While WO in his capacity as racing manager was preparing a Speed Six for the 1929 Le Mans, others had been convinced that only supercharging would produce the necessary increase in power. "Tim" Birkin – probably aided and abetted by Barnato – was so convinced of this that he had a 4½ Litre converted in his own workshops, and used it with some success that year although not at Le Mans.

WO, however, was firmly against supercharging and the stresses it imposed on an engine, and preferred to increase power by developing the larger engine more gradually. There was no sign of financial restraint at Cricklewood during this

period, with development of the Speed Six going ahead at the same time as new workshops and a new drawing office were being built (and presumably paid for). More than this, funds were also being committed to the development of yet another model, this time intended clearly for the carriage trade. This was the magnificent 8 Litre, effectively an enlarged version of the 6½ Litre, producing over 200bhp. It was a huge car, with wheelbase dimensions of either 142 or 156 inches, and it was aimed at the heart of the market occupied by such cars as the Rolls-Royce Phantom and the Daimler Double-Six.

When 1930 arrived it became clear that there was a split in the Bentley management. While WO

Le Mans 1929: Birkin brings the winning Speed Six home, closely followed by the other three team cars.

Another Freestone & Webb saloon, this time on a 1930 Speed Six chassis. "Float" style running boards were a fashion at the time.

Built for Woolf Barnato, this is a Gurney Nutting 2-seater (and dickey) body on 1930 4½ Litre supercharged chassis SM 3909.

occupied himself both with readying the 8 Litre model for sale and with preparing a team of Speed Sixes for Le Mans, Barnato and Birkin were pursuing quite different ideas. Birkin had found what he called a "fairy godmother" in the form of the Hon Dorothy Paget, whose prime interest in horse-racing he had managed to subvert towards motor sport. She bought his 4½ Litre cars and built a workshop at Welwyn Garden City, where Birkin set about converting the cars to supercharged models. He too was aiming at Le Mans, but for his entry to be accepted he needed to show that a minimum of fifty cars were under construction. This he left to Barnato, who organised a suitable production run at Cricklewood; just what WO thought of these developments can only be imagined. Birkin was thus clear to progress his own –

or rather Dorothy Paget's – Le Mans entry with the supercharged cars, apparently in competition with the works team.

In the end there was cooperation rather than competition at Le Mans, and in the end WO was right. Both the supercharged cars went out with engine trouble, but luckily so did Carraciola's Mercedes (also supercharged), allowing the two surviving works Speed Sixes to finish first and second. So it was yet another win for Bentley – and their last for many decades, as soon afterwards the company announced that it was ceasing its racing activities. The explanation at the time centred on the fact that they had achieved all they wanted to, and on the face of it one could see their point. With the advantage of hindsight, however, it suggests that the directors had at last woken up to

Le Mans 1930: the winning Speed Six (No 4), driven by Barnato and Kidston, here follows the Clement/Watney car which finished second.

The ultimate Cricklewood Bentley, a magnificent saloon on the 8 Litre long-wheelbase chassis.

the possibility of an economic depression hurting their sales.

The world economy was clearly in recession, and getting worse rather than better. Its effect was worse by far in the United States than in any other industrialised country – more severe, and more rapid. To take the motor industry as a particular example, production halved in the space of two years from 4 million units in 1929 to 1.9 million in 1931. By contrast Britain seemed to be riding out the storm more easily, and this undoubtedly gave rise to complacency in many boardrooms. Certainly the British motor industry fared much better, with a drop in production of only some 15% in the same period. However this overall figure conceals what was happening in certain segments: coachbuilding, for example or – most relevant to Bentley – small manufacturers of specialist cars. In this sector there was a sudden and dramatic drop in sales, which in due course led to many firms going out of business.

It is likely that just such a drop in sales was what the directors were looking at when they decided to pull out of racing. It was unfortunate that they had not spotted the trend a few months earlier, when there was still time to cancel the 8 Litre project. As it was, the 8 Litre went ahead although it was exactly the sort of car one would not want to launch at the start of an economic recession. It was previewed by the motoring press in September, and duly appeared at the following month's Olympia Show. Its combination of luxury and performance attracted a great deal of interest,

even at a chassis price of £1850, and numerous coachbuilders used the new chassis to display their wares on their own stands. Judging by subsequent delivery dates, sales got off to what was a reasonable start in the circumstances.

In the meantime, though, there were signs of panic in the boardroom. In the belief that their product offering was becoming too expensive for the market conditions, the directors went into reverse and demanded a new, cheaper model. This became known as the 4 Litre, which was to have a six-cylinder pushrod ohv engine mounted in a shortened version of the 8 Litre chassis. WO protested that he knew nothing about pushrods, so that part of the design was sub-contracted to Harry Ricardo's organisation. The result was an engine with an overhead inlet, side exhaust layout, and a chassis price of £1225.

The intention was clearly to compete with the smaller Rolls-Royce, the 20/25, and give Bentley, like Rolls-Royce, an each-way bet; if there was a move towards smaller, less luxurious cars, the 4 Litre would fill the bill, but if things turned out better than expected then the 8 Litre would sell well. This strategy might have worked if there had been time to design the new car from scratch and not modify an existing chassis. Unfortunately the 8 Litre chassis was a particularly heavy design, fine for the purpose for which it was intended but highly unsuitable as the basis for the smaller car. As a result the 4 Litre was heading for trouble from early on, being both overweight and underpowered.

Chapter Two

The Events of 1931

At the start of 1931 the Bentley company was in trouble. Sales of the 8 Litre, although better than might have been expected, were not enough to keep the company going. Meanwhile the new 4 Litre was not due for launch for several months, and its production required considerable expenditure on manufacturing facilities, thus using up the company's precious cash resources. In January two new outside directors joined the board, presumably in the hope that they could perform a financial miracle. Also in that month, the company made an approach to Rolls-Royce, although nothing came of it.

The 4 Litre was duly announced in May, and its reception amongst customers and competitors alike was poor. Rolls-Royce had been awaiting the new model with some trepidation since it was intended to take sales from the 20/25. However, a memo in the Rolls-Royce archives, from Arthur Sidgreaves (managing director) to Sir Henry Royce, sums up their feelings: "Bentley 4 Litre: I was interested to read your [report] on the above. We, as you know, heard glowing accounts of this prior to its appearance and as we knew that it was being brought out as a definite competitor of the 20/25, we naturally feared that it might prove rather a severe competitor. Since we have seen the car, however, we all feel considerably relieved."

The Bentley directors were now facing up to total financial disaster. No doubt they had assumed all along that Barnato would come to the rescue, even though he had tried to make it clear the previous year that he would not make any further

investment in the company. In the end he did not budge; when the insurance company London Life asked for their £65,000 loan to be repaid, Barnato refused to take over the obligation, and on 10 July London Life applied to put in a Receiver. Only some half-dozen 4 Litres had been delivered; the new car had failed to save the company.

It would seem that the Receiver, Patrick Raper Frere, was just the sort of person who should have been running the company in the first place. He got on well with both WO and the workforce, and managed to maintain morale during what was obviously a very difficult period. Meanwhile he was managing the company's financial affairs with some skill. When a company in the public eye crashes spectacularly in this manner, there is usually no need to go out and find buyers – they make the first approach. Within a short space of time, Frere was contacted by an ideal buyer: the Napier company.

Napier had been motor manufacturers both before and after World War One, producing expensive, quality cars which were regarded as competitors to the Rolls-Royce. However in 1924 they had taken the decision to withdraw from car manufacturing and concentrate on aero engines. Their Lion engine had gained a first-class reputation during the War and was still being produced, although now becoming a rather obsolete design. What particularly concerned Napier was that orders for new aero engines of any design were becoming hard to come by, with government contracts apparently ruled out for the foreseeable

May 1931: Woolf Barnato is ceremonially pulled home after his wedding, in his 8 Litre Freestone & Webb limousine, chassis YF 5010.

future. The company had tried and failed to negotiate a merger with Gloster Aircraft, and now badly needed a new source of business. A venture into the production of "mechanical horse" railway freight tugs was not going to be the whole answer, and the board decided that they would have to return to car manufacture, despite the heavy investment required.

The sudden availability of the Bentley company, or at least its assets, was the answer to their prayers. They could negotiate to purchase not only the name and the remaining cars, but importantly the services of WO himself; his design skills and up-to-date knowledge would speed up the timetable enormously. He was under a long-term service contract with the old company, and although it would not have been realistic to force him to serve out its terms, negotiation and persuasion would show him the benefits of doing so. Negotiations with Frere therefore began, apparently on a very friendly basis. Assuming that he had found the ideal buyer, Frere permitted a great

Another of Barnato's cars - a 4 Litre H J Mulliner Weymann saloon on chassis VF 4004, delivered in May 1931.

Napier's cars, like this splendid 40/50, were regarded as of similar quality to Rolls-Royce, but they ceased manufacturing them in 1924.

deal of informal cooperation while the terms of the deal were hammered out. This included WO working secretly on a new design at the Napier Works at Acton, and even the transfer of the remaining 8 Litre chassis there. Napier even began to clear an area of the works to prepare for production of the new car.

It was inevitable that some news of the impending deal would leak out, and it was probably naïve of Napier to assume that it could be kept secret. Sure enough, on 14 August a report appeared in *The Autocar* which revealed what was going on. "For some weeks past negotiations have been proceeding between D Napier & Son, Ltd, Acton, the famous aero engine manufacturers and Bentley Motors Ltd . . . [They have] reached an advanced stage, but nothing definite has been settled." Then came the news in late September that Bentley was going to be wound up, which would have alerted outside parties to the fact that an agreement was close. The outcome of the story is by now very well known. Court approval of the deal, which was going to cost Napier £103,675, was necessary, and in November 1931 the Receiver applied for that approval. To everyone's astonishment there was an intervention by counsel representing "The British Central Equitable Trust". After a rather unseemly process of sealed bids it turned out that this latter party had won the day with a bid of £125,256, greatly disappointing Napier who had only raised their bid by £1100. And the Trust, it transpired some days later, was acting on behalf of Rolls-Royce.

What were Rolls-Royce's motivations in buying Bentley? No-one from this distance can be entirely sure, but it seems likely that several reasons in combination led to the move. Firstly, Rolls-Royce were desperately afraid of the 8 Litre Bentley, and did not want to see it continue in production. They were far from complacent about competition, and had tracked the Bentley company's products for some years, but the 8 Litre was a direct attack on their flagship product, the Phantom II. A letter from Hives (at that time in charge of the Experimental department) to Royce, dated April 1931, makes the point clearly: "Mr Jack Barclay, one of our agents, had pointed out that it was difficult for him to sell a Continental Model against the Sports Bentley. He stated that the Sports Bentley with a comfortable saloon body would do 100mph . . . [There follows details of two Rolls-Royce experimental cars and two Bentleys, tested at Brooklands.] . . . If anything, the Bentley bodies were more roomy than ours . . .

	¼-mile mph	Lap speed mph
27-EX	84.9	83.7
26-EX	83.5	83.0
Bentley 6½ Litre	90	87.2
Bentley 8 Litre	99	97

. . . Summary: The 8 Litre Bentley is the best competitive car we have tried . . . At a genuine 75mph the absence of any roar or fuss was very remarkable in comparison with the Maybach 12 cyl."

Secondly, Rolls-Royce were also afraid of Napier. That company had already shown years before that

it could turn out a car which was as good as a Rolls-Royce, and there was every probability that it would do so again, especially with WO's expertise added in. More than that, Napier were also their closest competitors on the aero engine front, and the re-establishment of a successful car business would make them much stronger financially. Snatching Bentley from under their nose would thus spoil Napier's chances twice over.

Thirdly, there is the question of Rolls-Royce's overall strategy. If the first two reasons for purchasing Bentley were the only ones, they would have had no incentive to keep the name going. Yet all the evidence is that they began planning some sort of new Bentley as soon as they knew that their bid had been accepted. This implies that they saw the very existence of a second brand name as a positive advantage; for all we know it could have been a hot subject of debate within Rolls-Royce long before Bentley became available. What we do know is that they were unhappy with the limitations of their existing two-model policy, and were already developing a smaller model, the Peregrine project. Although it might have been a piece of serendipity, the sudden arrival of the Bentley name, and the reputation it brought with it, opened up new possibilities for expanding their product range.

Whatever the reasons for their bid, Rolls-Royce won the day, and in due course the assets the Trust had purchased on their behalf were transferred to a new company, Bentley Motors (1931) Limited. One of these assets was something of a curiosity:

the service contract between WO and the company, which presumably contained a clause binding him to any successor. There is evidence that Rolls-Royce took the contract on board with some reluctance; "it was necessary to take over the agreement", in the words of Sidgreaves' report to the Board. Some have queried why this should have been so, but the probability is that Napier had insisted that the contract was included in the package of assets for which they were negotiating. Thus when the sealed bid process began, Rolls-Royce were forced to bid for exactly the same package.

This was not the end of the story. A service contract is difficult to enforce without the cooperation of the individual involved, as both Rolls-Royce and Napier would have known. Early the following year WO made an attempt to break his ties with Rolls-Royce and move to Napier. Rolls-Royce were concerned but clearly felt they would be unable to retain him, as a letter from Sidgreaves to Royce (7 April 1932) confirms: "It is practically certain that WO Bentley is going to Napier's, and it is most important that we should make every effort to have our car out ahead of theirs." As things turned out, WO's effort failed and he remained with Rolls-Royce for several years.

When the Rolls-Royce board looked more carefully at what they had bought, they found that they had quite a bargain on their hands. The assets they took over, quite apart from intangibles such as the name and WO's contract, would have been buildings, machinery, work-in-progress, spares,

Yet another of Woolf Barnato's fleet, this time an 8 Litre with drophead coupé coachwork by Vanden Plas. Chassis YR 5095 of June 1931.

Royal visit: Prince George, Duke of York (later King George VI) inspects a Rolls-Royce 20/25hp at the Derby works in August 1931.

demonstration cars and so on. Sidgreaves had calculated that these were worth some £116,000, which meant that he would be paying a mere £9000 for the goodwill. After the event he was able to report that asset sales had in many cases exceeded estimate, so the Bentley name probably came to Rolls-Royce for a very small net cost indeed. The service station business was kept going, and was expected to be profitable.

The London Life Association were of course repaid in full, since their loan was a mortgage and therefore took precedence. The same applied to Barnato, whose 1929 mortgage of £35,000 was also repaid. Preference shareholders received a moderate payout, but ordinary creditors – always the last in line – received a mere 6d (2.5p) in the pound.

It was one thing for Rolls-Royce to get their hands on the Bentley business, but it was quite another for them to decide what to do with it. From the outset it is clear that there were different factions within the company propounding very different views. Some wanted to adapt the Peregrine project even though this would probably mean developing a supercharged version. Others,

with Hives vocal amongst them, were fearful of the development time that such a route would take, and proposed simpler and quicker ways of putting a car on the market. Meanwhile a third body of opinion wanted to write the specification of the new sports car from scratch, and proposed either the Alfa Romeo or the Lagonda as examples of what the company should be aiming at. Already by 4 December Royce was excitedly reporting that he and Elliott (head of engine design) had "schemed a smaller and improved G1 which is practically the same as the Alfa Romeo". (The "G1" reference is to an early scheme for the 20hp Rolls-Royce using an overhead camshaft engine.)

There was not even agreement as to where any new Bentley model should fit into the overall company strategy. This is very evident in the minutes of a meeting Wormald called on the last day of 1931, primarily in response to a letter from Hives to Sidgreaves and others a few days earlier, asking for help in defining the specification of the new car. Hives was pessimistic about the performance potential of anything based on the Peregrine project, with its small 2364cc engine, and assumed from the outset that it would need supercharging.

His overriding point is that he already had a suitable engine available – Project J (or " Japan") 1, a development of the existing 20/25 Rolls-Royce engine – which could be installed in the Peregrine chassis and would greatly cut down the long development time that a supercharged engine would require.

Wormald's conference tended to side with Hives. "The supercharged B.II" [the code name for the Peregrine-engined project] "will be a fast sporting car but the general opinion is that it will be decidedly unpleasant with a closed body and that this will reduce the size of the market considerably. The unsupercharged B.II will carry a closed body satisfactorily, but it has the objection that it will be exactly the same size and capacity, and have practically the same performance as the Peregrine. We are pushing ahead with both these models of B.II, but would like to add a further model to be made for experimental test. It was suggested and agreed that it be recommended" [note the tortuous language to take account of office politics] "that we take the B.II chassis minus engine unit and fit to it the improved J.1 engine unit. This combination would give a compact fast sporting car which would be pleasant to use with a closed body, and it is anticipated that it would do 90mph."

Sidgreaves was having none of this. Responding a few days later from his London vantage point, he used both his own views and those of William Cowen, the head of sales, to try and stifle the J.1 engine project at birth. They both expressed the fear that such a car would have to be priced at the same level as the Rolls-Royce 20/25 and would eat directly into sales of that model. Cowen went further, specifying that the new Bentley should attack the 18hp class and sell for under £1000. Interestingly, Cowen gives one of the few clear statements of the company's reasons for buying Bentley: "The first idea of keeping alive the name of Bentley was (a) to endeavour to make use of the goodwill created by the name amongst sporting drivers; (b) to endeavour to use that goodwill in getting more chassis work into Derby." Someone within the company then leaked the discussion to the press, who duly reported that the new Bentley would have a 2500cc engine which would be offered both with and without a supercharger.

So Hives was forced to put his J.1 project aside for the time being and work on the supercharged Peregrine engine in spite of his misgivings. Interestingly, if the J.1 route had been authorised immediately it would have produced a car not very different from the one which was eventually launched – and almost a year earlier.

Numerous 8 Litre chassis were bodied and sold after the receivership. This Lancefield tourer on chassis YM 5044 was not completed until May 1932.

Chapter Three

Birth of the 3½ Litre

T he Peregrine project was a direct response to the Depression. At a time when money was very tight and even those with money did not want to be accused of extravagance, the Rolls-Royce two-model line-up of Phantom II (chassis price £1750) and 20/25 (chassis price £1050) was hardly the most appropriate. The 20 horsepower range had been introduced partly to cater for the "owner-driver" type of customer, but over the years it had grown in complication and cost to the point where it was more often chauffeur-driven. There was a need for a model that was

Sir Henry Royce, the genius behind Rolls-Royce design, who died before the first Derby Bentley went on sale.

smaller and less expensive than the 20/25, but which was still built to Rolls-Royce's high standards.

By the time that Bentley Motors (1931) had been formed, Peregrine was an established project with engine and chassis design already approved. The engine was a conventional six-cylinder design with overhead valves operated by pushrods. Cylinder dimensions were 2.725 x 4.125in bore and stroke, giving a cubic capacity of 2366cc. One feature new for a Rolls-Royce engine was that there were no water passages through the head gasket. The chassis was of conventional design, with leaf springs all round and a wheelbase of 120in – 12in shorter than the 20/25. There is a suggestion, unconfirmed, that the design also incorporated a separate sub-frame for the engine.

Peregrine was in many ways an obvious starting point from which to develop a new Bentley. Importantly, its shorter wheelbase meant that it would pose little threat to the 20/25 model and none at all to the Phantom; Rolls-Royce had no intention of developing the sort of competitor which the 8 Litre Bentley had represented. Its engine, however, posed more of a problem, since as it stood it was unlikely ever to develop more than 70bhp. This would be more than adequate for the rather staid four-passenger saloon which the company envisaged as its new small Rolls-Royce, capable of taking the car up to 70mph and beyond, but it was nowhere near enough for a sports car carrying the Bentley name, where at least 110bhp would be needed.

The immediate thought, as we have seen, was to add a supercharger to the Peregrine engine. In January 1932 Royce himself was quite adamant about this, stating that the J.1 engine should be reserved for the 20/25 (later 25hp) Rolls-Royce. "It should be understood by all that the best we can do should be reserved for RR, and thus J.1 or J.3 will be the RR continental tourer. We are obliged to have something quite different to RR for the 'Bensport' – ie extra low frame, small weight, and head resistance, so that 'Peregrine' size engine, supercharged, giving 90/100hp, will make it perform well with low tax.".

Yet by March doubts were creeping in. Out of the blue Royce proposed that, to get over the problems which supercharging would bring, the Peregrine engine should be increased in capacity by turning it into a straight-eight, retaining the same cylinder dimensions. Sidgreaves' response to the idea starts diplomatically by describing it as "very attractive technically", but then proceeds to demolish it. He points out, quite rightly, that such a car would turn out to be more expensive than the 20/25hp Rolls-Royce "which is just what we do not

The Rolls-Royce "Peregrine" project had an 18hp, 2366cc engine, and was intended to provide a smaller and cheaper alternative to the 20/25hp.

Far left: Arthur Sidgreaves, later knighted, Rolls-Royce managing director. Left: Ernest (later Lord) Hives, head of the Experimental department during the development of the Derby Bentley

The Rolls-Royce 20/25hp. A modified version of its engine went into the 3½ Litre Bentley.

want". The last part of his letter reveals the type of car he personally has in mind. "You will remember that, when we first bought the Alfa Romeo, I said quite definitely that we did not want a car of that type but we wanted something to compete more with the Lagonda, Talbot and Alvis type of sports car."

He continues: "I agree that the engine will be on the small side but we are all quite sure that, by keeping it to this size and class and price of car we shall get into a very much bigger market whereas, if we were to allow it to become an 8 cylinder, we should automatically go into a very much smaller market, and I am afraid really that the whole scheme would be a failure unless the design is such as to enable the factory to produce a car, the chassis of which can be sold retail at round about £600 to £700. We can buy bodies in quantities of quite a good type for a car of this description for about £100 each, and the price I have always had in mind for the complete car is round about £750 without the supercharger." The problem Sidgreaves does not address, however, is how he would change the prevailing perfectionist attitude within Rolls-Royce. Only if the inevitable compromises in design and production were accepted could he achieve such a price.

While engine options were being discussed, including an overhead cam version of Peregrine, it would appear that work was progressing steadily on the design of the chassis. In March the wheelbase was lengthened by an inch without changing the basic chassis design, by the simple expedient

of moving the front axle forward on the springs. It seems, incidentally, that this change was to give clearance for the supercharger. During May it became evident that the wheelbase should be even longer, and the dimension was increased by another three inches to 10ft 4in. While informing the production side, Day (chief chassis designer) somewhat defensively points out that "the new Alvis Speed Twenty, one of our most serious competitors, has a wheelbase of 10 feet 3 inches". Otherwise it appears that every effort was being made to retain as much commonality as possible between the two chassis, Peregrine and Bensport. Later (August) a memo from Royce to Elliott and Hives confirms a further lengthening to 10ft 6in, and makes it clear that the change was to accommodate the front mounting position of the supercharger.

Meanwhile, the reservations which Hives had always held about supercharging were beginning to be shared by others. Elliott reported to Royce on a visit from Capt G E T Eyston, who acted for the supercharger manufacturers Powerplus. Eyston had emphasised the need for superchargers to be constantly lubricated, and recommended adding oil to the petrol. Needless to say, the idea of asking a customer to carry out this routine was highly unattractive to any Rolls-Royce man. Eyston furthermore intimated that the Alfa Romeo supercharged engines, particularly the eight-cylinder, were known to be unreliable. Elliott speculated that the company might have to look at the Roots supercharger instead.

Increasingly one gains the feeling from this correspondence that time is being lost, and that the cause is an inability on the part of various individuals to make up their minds. Mostly, it must be said, the finger must be pointed at Royce's base at West Wittering, where his failing health was making him less decisive than before when faced with a choice between possible technical solutions. Some of the delay, nevertheless, could be laid at the door of the London management, who were still trying to decide exactly what sort of Bentley they wanted. To help them, they tried out various competitors during the course of 1932, including the Alvis Speed 20 and two different supercharged Alfa Romeos, the 2300 straight-eight and the 1750 six-cylinder.

The Alvis seems to have received special attention, no doubt because Sidgreaves had singled it out as the closest match to what he was trying to achieve. In the latter part of May two different senior Rolls-Royce employees – Day and Cox (head of sales in London) – managed to obtain test drives, both in open tourer models. Their subsequent reports were highly complimentary about the car's performance and handling, but less so about such areas as ride comfort, engine smoothness and gearbox noise – areas to which Rolls-Royce traditionally paid particular attention. Day went so far as to propose that "Derby should try one of these cars if they have not already done so, and put it through their normal tests". It would appear that his suggestion was taken up, although not until some months had elapsed.

Peregrine, meanwhile, had reached the stage of a roadworthy car. It gave a good initial impression as far as the directors were concerned, but subsequent testing in continental Europe began to show up its limitations. These particularly concerned the

The Rolls-Royce Phantom II. Falling sales of their larger model partly motivated the company's acquisition of the Bentley name.

1932 Alvis Speed 20. The new Bentley was intended to compete against this type of sports car.

Lagonda M45 on the Monte Carlo rally. This car, more expensive than the Alvis, was to become an even closer competitor to the Bentley

engine bearings, which were constantly being replaced during what was supposed to be a 10,000-mile test. The basic problem was one of crankshaft vibration, which reached its critical period at just over 5000rpm. Unfortunately it was proving necessary to use such engine speeds in order to produce the required performance. Would even this model have to have a supercharger?

Royce and Elliott continued to debate alternative engine arrangements for the Bentley. Royce at this point was in favour of using a single overhead camshaft, in order to give it a different appearance from the Peregrine version. Apparently the sales department were afraid that if Bensport finished up very similar to Peregrine there would be no excuse for a difference in price. Hives queried this approach, and suggested alternative ways of differentiating the two engines. Elliott, however, was more concerned with the mounting of the supercharger. This would now have to be at the side of the engine, as tests with it mounted in front had shown up problems with the fuel supply.

Time was moving on, and Hives's patience was clearly running out. At the end of September he went into print with what was clearly intended to be a major critique of the Bensport project. In it he described progress so far with the supercharged Peregrine engine, and listed the problems his team had found so far. These included detonation, which could only be solved by lowering the compression ratio; head gasket leaks, which would require a total redesign to increase the distance between the bores; supercharger lubrication, which could only be provided satisfactorily by adding oil to the petrol; and excessive supercharger temperatures. Hives observed that they were a long way from finding a satisfactory supercharger, and that it might well be necessary for the company to design its own. He also noted that Lagonda, who were formerly strong proponents of superchargers, had now omitted them from their model line-up.

The remainder of the report was a reasoned recommendation to return to the J.1 engine. "This engine gives us the same power as our best anticipated figure for the Bensport . . . If we picture the two cars we have Bensport with its sensitive engine including the supercharger. It will be essential to use special oil, it will be essential to always remember to add oil to the petrol (if this is not done the supercharger may be destroyed), and we are certain to have a fussy car. The tax of this car would be £18. The alternative car with J.1 would be an engine of proved reliability and quality. It

The Talbot was another competitor to contend with, and it had a formidable competition record. Here the 1934 Alpine Rally team 105s line up at Nice.

Experimental chassis 4-B-IV was fitted with a Park Ward tourer body, but it was not adopted as a standard coachwork design.

would give the same power but would do it in a very much pleasanter way ... In our opinion it would be a car of outstanding quality, whereas if we make a supercharged car, unless we are going to make it very different to any supercharged car which has yet been made it will be simply a fast car." Finally, although Hives conceded that his proposed car would be in a higher tax bracket – £26 instead of £18 per annum – he pointed out that this would be offset by better fuel consumption. He emphasised that the project was ready and waiting, and that it could be regarded as an interim product pending the development of the supercharged engine. "In the meantime if we leave the Bentley Co. without a car to sell the goodwill must disappear."

Hives's letter was addressed to Sidgreaves but was copied to many others (with the notable exception of Royce himself). It would appear that the whole exercise was conducted in collusion with Sidgreaves, who intended to force a decision from Royce but who wanted to obtain maximum support beforehand. Such support was immediately forthcoming from Elliott, whose response included a table forecasting the performance of a J.1-powered car. Making assumptions about maximum brake horsepower and also the frontal area of different bodies, he predicted maximum speeds of 89mph for the Bensport saloon and 102mph for the open sports.

From now on the plot becomes clear. A memo from Sidgreaves to Wormald is worth quoting in full as it typifies the tortuous decision process

under which the company had to operate: "Referring to [Hives's memo] and our lengthy discussion on the subject yesterday, I was thinking afterwards that, before we act on the decision come to, ie to put the J.1 engine out of 19-G-IV into a Bensport chassis, we ought to put a memo up to R [Royce] on the subject, and I suggest that Hs [Hives] should write a memo, utilising the greater part of his memo quoted above, refer to the fact that it was discussed at a full conference at Derby, etc. etc., and put it up in such a way as not actually to ask for approval but to infer that "silence will give consent".

Silence there was, for two whole weeks, before Royce responded. He thought that Hives's idea of applying the J.1 engine to the Bensport chassis was "very good indeed", but then rather spoilt the effect by continuing to discuss the supercharged engine. However since Hives had not suggested cancelling work on this latter project, the Derby management took Royce's reaction as agreement, and work began at full speed to install the J.1 engine in the modified Peregrine chassis. We can only assume that by this time the Experimental department had already procured a chassis to the latest 10ft 6in wheelbase, or had modified a standard Peregrine one themselves, as otherwise the J.1 engine would not have fitted into the available space. We must further assume that, if there had indeed been a sub-frame for the Peregrine engine, then this item would have been omitted in order to give sufficient space for the J.1 engine.

The engine itself was based on the then current 20/25 unit, with the same cylinder dimensions but with a different head of cross-flow design which entailed major modifications to the induction system. At a later stage of development it also acquired twin SU carburettors instead of the single one of Rolls-Royce manufacture. Other changes were an increased compression ratio, new connecting rods and altered cam profiles. In order to install it in the Bensport chassis some further modifications had to be made, including a different crankcase and a revised front engine mounting. It also seems that at this stage a dry sump set-up was being proposed.

Even though Hives was now trying to go flat out there were hold-ups, which no doubt he found particularly frustrating. These mainly concerned the gearbox, since the modified Peregrine gearbox – which the new Bentley was intended to use – was still being designed. In the meantime he and others had been trying out the competition a little more. Evernden, the coachwork design specialist at West Wittering, reported on a test drive in the Alvis Speed Twenty Thrupp & Maberly four-door saloon. Although reasonably complimentary, he summarised by saying "there is little doubt that Bensport will be an infinitely better car with much greater refinement, and a much better performance in that its engine is 3660cc, or 40% bigger." Already confidence had increased now that their car was a known quantity, but did Evernden think that the Bentley selling price would be anywhere near to the Alvis's £895?

On 18 January 1933 Hives was at last able to report to Royce that the first Bensport mock-up had been run on the road. It had the 20/25 gearbox as a temporary measure, and Hives noted that he expected to wait another two months for the correct gearbox. The chassis had been fitted with a Park Ward saloon body. Five days later he reported on a trip he and his assistant Robotham had made in the car to West Wittering and back (which was probably the one and only time Royce was to see a Derby-built Bentley). Although Hives could hardly have been described as unbiased, it is obvious that he is delighted with his new creation. "This car, as it is with a mock-up J.1 unit, on its first run, is far better than any sports car which is being sold today". They managed to reach an indicated 95mph on occasion, and Hives estimated that the true measured maximum speed would be about 85mph. He is particularly full of praise for the steering, the brakes, and the quietness and smoothness of the engine. However he then qualifies this last point by saying that the "master crank period" could be felt at 70mph in third gear (the equivalent of about 4500rpm). This is the first mention of a problem which would occupy much of his time during the development of both this car and its successors.

Hives now played his master stroke. In a further report dated only nine days later, he firstly made it clear that all the relevant managers thought that the current Bensport was "a very desirable motorcar, and one that should be got on to production as soon as possible". He then pointed out that, if they had to wait another two or three months for the new gearbox (together with modified clutch and crankcase) plus at least two months of proving trials, they would have no hope of getting a production car ready for exhibition at the next Olympia Show in October. "If we are to do anything with the Bentley business we must exhibit a car at next Olympia and the only chance

Unlike the first Vanden Plas tourers the Park Ward boasted a spare wheel cover, but it lacked the VdP's domed and valanced front wings.

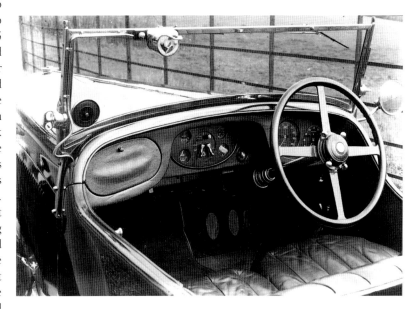

The interior of 4-B-IV, the Park Ward tourer

of doing that is to accept the car as it stands." He then sugars the pill – just as he did with the super-charger project – by saying that of course this does not stop development work continuing on the new gearbox.

Yet another memo a few days later from Hives, to Wormald and Sidgreaves, appears to be a follow-up to some intensive discussions. It marks a crucial step in the company's understanding of the sort of Bentley car they could and could not make, and in the positioning which the Bentley marque was to acquire in the market place. Hives wants to make it clear that a "cheap" Bentley was just not possible, since it would be made largely of Rolls-Royce 20/25 parts which would be manufactured to the usual high Rolls-Royce standards. Indeed, since the car would be of higher performance than the 20/25 some of those parts might even have to be of superior quality. He finishes: "Our recommendation is that we should make the car as good as we know how and then charge accordingly. It is very much easier for us to make a thing good than it is for us to make it cheap. We know in making the car good we are on safe ground, but if we attempt to do anything else we have no experience to follow." In other words, this was the point when the company realised that it was temperamentally unsuited to producing a car at the price of the Alvis Speed Twenty or Talbot 105, or even of the Lagonda.

Now that the final specification was settled, the emphasis was on testing, using initially the so-called "mock-up" car. This car, known officially as 1-B-III but more commonly referred to as Bensport 3 or B3, was for some months the only experimental car, and it led a hard life in consequence. In early February it was at Brooklands for maximum speed tests, and Hives reported that it lapped at 87mph normally, or at 89mph if the exhaust cut-out was used. It appears to have been on this same occasion that WO Bentley joined senior sales staff to try the car. His report made a number of constructive comments, but finished with words that have become part of Bentley history: "Taking all things in consideration I would rather own this Bentley car than any car produced under that name".

B3 now started on intensive road-testing on the Continent, a normal Rolls-Royce practice. It went out first during February with Robotham in charge, and on its return it immediately went out again, this time for WO Bentley to test. It was probably on this second run, in April, that the car suffered a broken piston, since this apparently occurred at 12,000 miles. The fault was subsequently blamed on the wrong material having been used, but at the same time the design was changed to eliminate circlips on the gudgeon pins. Further experimental cars were badly needed, and four such chassis had been laid down, but with their production suffering constant minor amendments the first car did not emerge until April, and the last in July. These cars bore the designations 1-B-IV to 4-B-IV.

The refinements which had to be tested were numerous, covering such things as ignition timing, induction and exhaust systems, brakes, petrol pumps and rear axles. At one stage a three-carburettor set-up was even under consideration, but this idea seems to have been dropped quite quickly. By this time – March or April – it would appear that dry sump lubrication had been abandoned, as had radiator shutters (replaced by an in-line thermostat). Where possible, the Experimental department used two local hills, Ticknall

Hill and Pistern Hill, for their tests, since they had built up a body of standard times with which to compare. For maximum speed runs, however, it was usually necessary to measure a flying lap at Brooklands, where again the results could be compared with data built up over the years. In addition they of course carried out much static testing within the factory. After one such test, apparently on a rolling road dynamometer, Hives reported that 2-B-IV had produced 90.4bhp at the rear wheels. (This compares with a figure of 110bhp which the engine was probably producing "at the clutch" at that time).

April also marked the emergence of the new Bentley's name – 3½ Litre – which was to be used in all company correspondence from now on in place of Bensport. Commercial considerations were beginning to occupy everyone's thoughts, and the following month the Brooklands test programme included two competitors, a Talbot 95 saloon and an Alvis Speed Twenty tourer. These two lapped the track at average speeds of 82.3mph and 80.5mph respectively, as against 87.0 and 85.4 for the two Bentley experimental cars 1-B-IV and 2-B-IV (both saloons) with exhaust cut-out closed, a reassuring result for all concerned. A lap at Brooklands was by no means the same as testing the car's maximum speed, which was usually measured over a quarter or half mile of level road. For comparison, at this same test 1-B-IV achieved 93mph over the flying half mile – admittedly with the cut-out open, which would have equated to about 91mph with cut-out closed.

In May the pressures on the Experimental department were beginning to mount. Robotham wrote to Hives, his superior, listing ten important design points which were still unresolved and which needed testing either at Brooklands or in France. The induction system was giving most concern, since the carburettors, manifold heating, air silencer and petrol pump were all new and untested. It seems that at this stage both exhaust and water heating were being considered for the inlet manifold, and the choice had to be made quickly since orders had to be placed for the first production batch of cars. Robotham finishes with the pointed comment: "The proper Bentley [engine] unit with altered crankcase, new pistons, slow speed dynamo and altered starter motor housing has never been run in France, and we are ordering 200 sets of material".

Robotham's comment about a "slow speed dynamo" refers to another problem discovered

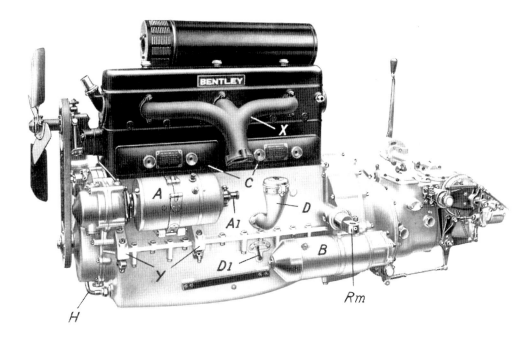

Nearside view of the engine and gearbox, showing the exhaust side of the cross-flow head.

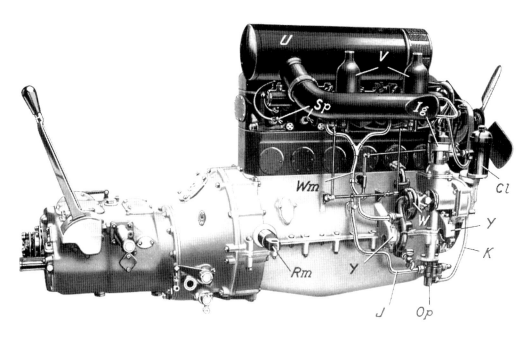

Offside view of the engine, showing the massive air cleaner/silencer feeding twin SU carburettors.

during development. The new Bentley engine was running at speeds which no normal Rolls-Royce engine had attained in the past. In testing at these speeds the dynamo, made by Rolls-Royce, was reaching some 7500rpm and was found to be overheating. There then followed a visit to Joseph Lucas, no doubt on the pretext of a possible order, where it became clear that Lucas would never allow a dynamo to run at more than 5000rpm. The consequence was that the gearing arrangement at the front of the Bentley engine had to undergo

modifications to slow down the dynamo.

More of the company's management were now being given the opportunity to drive the car. Platford, the chief tester, was in general highly complimentary, but was critical of fumes – presumed from the exhaust – in the interior. Others complained that the second test car was inferior to the first in respect of both maximum speed and "wander" in the steering. Sidgreaves was concerned about these differences, but also about the second car's quietness, which he blamed on the air silencer. "The car must have a sports harshness . . . instead of keeping it rough it seems to have become very RR-like." The important point, he emphasises, is "will we sell more 20/25's and B's collectively . . . than if we sold no B's at all? . . . For it not to affect to any serious extent the 20/25 sales we must have the higher speed, more noise and small bodies".

Bodywork matters were the subject of a conference called by Evernden at the end of May. From its minutes one can begin to perceive how much the company in general, and Evernden in particular, were driving the programme to produce standardised coachwork. For example, the open body fitted to the fourth experimental car was "not approved", and Evernden himself took responsibility for producing a new design. (Possibly this was behind the switch to Vanden Plas for the standard open body, Park Ward having supplied all four of the experimental bodies.) In similar vein, it was decided that the steel internal wheel arches would be supplied by the company, as "they are difficult to make and the coachbuilders will probably make a mess of the job if they have to produce them themselves". There was a strong desire expressed to keep down the weight of these bodies, with running boards weighing 60lb each coming in for particular criticism.

The Experimental department had their own opinions on current bodywork trends, not all of them complimentary. In particular Hives and Robotham were frustrated by carping from various quarters about maximum speeds, pointing out that these figures could be increased dramatically if customers could be persuaded to adopt more "streamlined" body styles. As part of this campaign they subjected different designs of front wing firstly to wind-tunnel tests (no doubt using the company's aircraft industry contacts) and then to track tests at Brooklands. These compared the so-called "flared" and "domed" designs of wing, where the latter shape came much further forward over the front of the wheel and also had side valances. The results showed that this simple change alone was worth an additional 2½mph on top speed. Hives was to return to this subject the following year.

It was now June 1933. Hives, still frantically engaged in proving tests on a car that was due to be launched in three months' time, had to extend his programme to prove or disprove the comments that were beginning to build up. One example was the air cleaner, where a special test at Brooklands confirmed what Hives already knew, namely that its presence made no difference to the car's maximum speed. As to the car being "too quiet", he wrote to Cowen with a well-reasoned reply, which finished: "We believe the right attitude is not to make the Bentley more noisy but to make the R.R. more silent, and in that way we should be making progress." He accepted that there was a difference in maximum speed between the No 1 and No 2 cars, but his response was to give a gentle lesson in statistics: "We cannot avoid these variations and we certainly cannot promise that all cars will be up to the standard of No 1 because to do this it would mean that all cars would have to be better than No 1". His final, barbed comment is also worth reproducing: "One noticeable point about our discussion was that no-one brought forward any ideas of any competitive car which had a better performance than the 3½ Litre Bentley".

In spite of the delay since the purchase of the Bentley company, public interest in the forthcoming "Rolls-Bentley" (as it was increasingly being described) was intense. A disadvantage of using the Brooklands track was that it was open to the public, so that total secrecy was impossible. In any case a certain amount of speculation would have been welcome, since the important thing was to keep the Bentley name alive. However the company cannot have been totally delighted when the magazine *Brooklands* described the experimental car in some detail, including the phrase "the engine is to all appearances a 'hotted up' 25hp Rolls-Royce with two carburettors". This was exactly the impression they were trying to avoid, and they intensified their efforts to disguise the common origin of parts wherever possible. Hives, with his usual prescience, gave his opinion that the "young fraternity . . . talk a lot, and they will undoubtedly express more or less disgust at our 3½ Litre car". To counter any such negative comment the company was clearly indulging in some deliberate leaking to build up interest. On 7 July the gossip column of *The Autocar* reported that "the new 3½ Litre Bentley will make its debut at the Show, where a separate stand has been taken for its exhibition", and then added, slightly mischievously, "it should be good considering the amount of time, thought and testing it has received".

During June the decision was taken to cease all work on the Peregrine project. This would undoubtedly have been welcome to many, as it allowed them to concentrate on the Bentley. Hives,

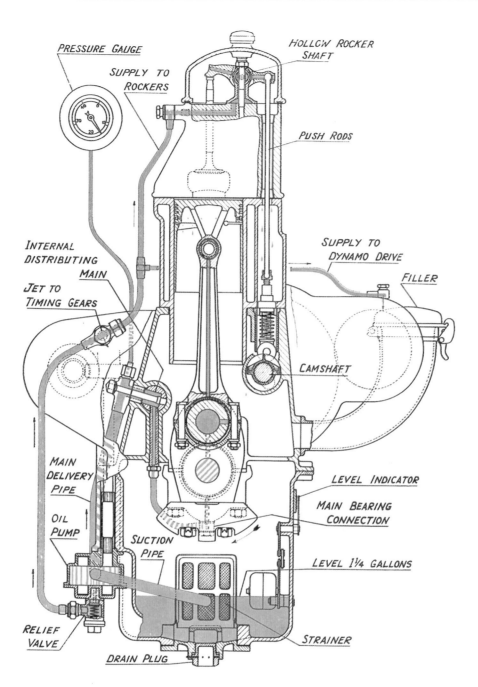

PRESSURE GAUGE

SUPPLY TO ROCKERS

HOLLOW ROCKER SHAFT

PUSH RODS

INTERNAL DISTRIBUTING MAIN

JET TO TIMING GEARS

SUPPLY TO DYNAMO DRIVE

FILLER

CAMSHAFT

MAIN DELIVERY PIPE

OIL PUMP

SUCTION PIPE

LEVEL INDICATOR

MAIN BEARING CONNECTION

LEVEL 1¼ GALLONS

RELIEF VALVE

DRAIN PLUG

STRAINER

Section of the 3½ Litre engine, with the lubrication system highlighted.

in particular, needed all the time he could get, as he had a serious problem on his hands: crankshaft vibration. This had surfaced in January during the prototype's first trip, when it became noticeable at 70mph in third gear. Now in July it occurred again in rather more spectacular fashion when Cox (of the London sales office) suffered severe engine vibration problems during a weekend of testing, which were traced to the "flywheel" coming loose. (The word "flywheel" in RR-speak could mean several things, including the vibration damper and even the crankshaft counterweights.) Hives's response encapsulates the typical engineer's view of salesmen, implying without stating that Cox must have over-revved the engine, and reassuring him that the production cars would be red-lined at 4500rpm. Sidgreaves however – less easily deceived – expressed serious concern and asked for more fundamental assurances. Within a week Hives had issued a programme of "modifications and improvements for the second series", which amongst numerous other items included a

Top: *One of the first production batch, chassis B15AE, with Park Ward saloon body. Note the full-height radiator with thermostatic shutters.* Above: *Chassis B1AE, with the Vanden Plas tourer body which was adopted as standard. Woolf Barnato is at the wheel.*

proposal to increase the crankshaft main bearing diameter by half an inch. "This will put up our critical speed approximately 150rpm and will provide an extra safeguard on any damage to the crankshaft." The implication of this change, incidentally, is that the Bentley crankshaft had not until then been brought up to the current specification of the 20/25hp Rolls-Royce, and was still using 1⅞in diameter main journals.

Even this proved not to be enough, and in September a very late change was made to the engine design, incorporating revisions to the crankshaft balance weights (known internally as the "Packard" system) and to the "flywheel securing bolts". Any urgent revisions at this point were serious, as the first 15 production examples were already being manufactured. Less urgent changes were planned to be fitted to the next batch, which

would be of 200 cars, although as things turned out virtually none of the revisions would have completed testing in time. The planned programme was for an announcement in the middle of September, in good time for the Olympia Show in October, and then for delivery of chassis to coachbuilders to start in the first week of November. Wormald was asking for an initial build rate of six per week, rising to ten per week as soon as possible thereafter. Everything looked promising – until the sales department put a spanner in the works.

Cowen dropped his bombshell on 24 August, only weeks away from the official launch. "I am afraid this may come as a bit of a shock to you", he starts in a letter to Wormald, "but I hope it won't in view of the fact that the appearance of the Bentley has been criticised at Derby recently. The fact of the matter is that everybody who has so far seen the Bentley chassis which we have delivered to the coachbuilders has criticised the radiator as looking cheap and undistinguished. Unfortunately I must confess that I agree with them, as from the beginning I have hated the idea of what is know as the 'wire stone screen'".

Early pictures of experimental cars show the radiator set-up to which Cowen was referring – a chromed shell surrounding a wire gauze, which acted as a stone guard in front of the radiator matrix. He supported his case with the views of the artist Gordon Crosby, who made similar, unprompted comments about the radiator when he was drawing the chassis for *The Autocar*, and Mr Pass of the dealers Pass & Joyce, who likened its cheap appearance to American practice (not a compliment in those days!). Cowen's proposed solution was simple – go back to polished radiator shutters. He realised this would also mean that they would have to be thermostatically controlled, and that this arrangement would replace the thermostat control in the cooling system

Even though he had touched a nerve, Cowen had not covered all the areas of criticism. There was also apparently a body of opinion which held that the radiator was too "squat" – which meant not deep enough. In a letter two days after Cowen's, Elliott proposed that the bottom edge of the radiator should be dropped by four inches, and that the front apron, which at that time bridged the space between the dumb-irons, should be deleted. Instead, separate valances should cover each dumb-iron and then curl round behind the radiator. The radiator shell and front gauze ("metal lacing") would be lengthened, but not the matrix

behind. These proposals – modified only by adding a horizontal apron, level with the bottom of the dumb irons – were promptly implemented on all existing and future chassis. Thus the imposing appearance of the Derby Bentley, which became such a familiar sight over the years, only came about at the last moment.

Significantly, Elliott's note made no mention of radiator shutters, and the engineering staff were no doubt fervently hoping that the idea would go away. On the contrary, however, thermostatically controlled radiator shutters became part of the launch specification, and were added not only to the first 15 production cars but also (of course) to the experimental cars in time for the press launch. Fortunately there had been some Continental testing of the set-up earlier in the year, and such problems as had shown up then could be solved relatively simply. This gave enough confidence for the time being, but the new arrangement was rapidly incorporated into the car on continental test.

Yet another suggestion to improve the car's frontal appearance was to add a radiator mascot. This was not a new idea: there had previously been an internal competition to design a suitable mascot, which had not produced an entry judged suitable. Instead, Charles Sykes (designer of the Rolls-Royce "Spirit of Ecstasy" mascot) had been commissioned to produce some proposals, and these were still under consideration when Elliott revived the subject. Elliott saw this as a means of increasing the apparent height of the radiator, without the complication of altering the radiator itself. "We feel that this question of a mascot should be followed up as the public will very likely expect something of this sort in the same way as the mascot used on the Roll-Royce cars has been regarded as representing the characteristics of the car." The suggestion was indeed followed up, but not in time, and there were no mascots on the cars at the time of the launch.

After the eleventh-hour changes had been made, all was now ready for the cars to be introduced to the public. What would their reaction be? Would the old Bentley clientele still be attracted to the new car, or would it appeal to an entirely new group of buyers? Did it have enough performance for the former, and if so would they feel that it was too quiet to be a real sports car? Would it eat into Rolls-Royce sales? Most importantly, at what price would the company pitch the car? Would it be too highly priced to win buyers from Alvis, Lagonda, Talbot and so on? Only time would tell.

Experimental chassis 2-B-IV, with Mrs Platford, wife of R-R's chief tester. Although the photo was taken some time after the model's launch, the car has retained the earlier design of "stoneguard" grille.

Chapter Four

The 3½ Litre

This photo and the three overleaf are of chassis B89CW, a 1935 Vanden Plas tourer. When first delivered the car was painted in two-tone silver and blue.

The car which was unveiled to the press at the end of September 1933 was in many ways a conventional design. The ladder-frame chassis carried axles suspended on semi-elliptic springs front and back, and the engine was a normally aspirated in-line six-cylinder with overhead valves operated by pushrods. Careful study, however, reveals numerous sophisticated features which together raise the design above the ordinary.

The nickel steel chassis, of 10ft 6in wheelbase, is a "double-dropped" layout – that is to say, the channel section side rails are raised at front and back to clear the axles. These rails are 6½in deep along their horizontal section but then taper rapidly as they pass over each axle. Compared

The forward cross-bracing for the chassis, above the apron joining the two wing valances, can be clearly seen. The Lalique glass mascot is a later - and very expensive - addition.

The front shock absorber arm is connected to the axle by a triangulated bracket which is designed to resist axle deflection under braking.

with other contemporary designs the chassis is noticeably light, having six tubular or channel-section cross-members and only two of girder design; there is no diagonal cross-bracing. Starting at the front, there is a tubular cross-member placed just behind the front spring shackles, and this also carries the forward end of the support tube for the starting handle. This is the member which, as we have seen, had to be exposed when the radiator was deepened just before the launch, and later in the model's life it was re-positioned (and strengthened) so that it was once again concealed by the front apron. Next, just behind the radiator, comes another tubular member which provides support for both the radiator and the front engine mounting. At the rear of the gearbox is a pressed steel cross-member which carries the rear mounting for the integral engine-gearbox unit. After this there is a stout tube, running below the propellor shaft, which acts as the anchorage for the brake equalisers. Next comes another deep pressed steel cross-member which ties the forward anchorage points of the rear springs, and which is cut away in the centre to allow the propellor shaft to pass through it. Three more cross-members tie the rear ends of the frame together, the last being located just forward of the rear spring shackles. Later, further strengthening was added near the front of the chassis to give more rigidity to the headlamp supports.

The springs are particularly long, especially at the rear, and special attention has been paid to the avoidance of inter-leaf friction, all the leaves being hollow ground, polished and cadmium plated. In addition the top four leaves are lubricated directly from the centralised chassis lubrication system, while the remaining leaves receive indirect lubrication from the excess oil held in the spring gaiters. These details ensure that damping of wheel movement is controlled almost entirely by the shock absorbers, which are hydraulic lever-arm type and of Rolls-Royce design and manufacture. The front ones are connected to the axle beam by a link in the form of an A-bracket, which also acts as a reaction member to counter braking torque – a system already in use on Rolls-Royce models of the time. The chassis is mounted on 18in wire wheels, originally with India Speed Special 18 x 5.50 tyres. Steering is via a Rolls-Royce steering box which uses a steel worm and a nut lined with white metal.

The engine is, as has been stated, an apparently conventional in-line six with two overhead valves per cylinder. Cylinder dimensions are 3¼in bore and 4½in stroke, giving a capacity of 3669cc and an RAC rating of 25.3hp. Both the block and the head are cast iron, whereas the crankcase, sump and clutch housing are of aluminium. The cylinder block is held by long studs which run right through from the head to the crankcase, thus sandwiching the block between the two. Pressed-in steel liners project some two inches into the crankcase below the block. A nickel chrome steel crankshaft, fully machined and balanced, runs in seven bearings of 2⅜in diameter. These bearings, in the form of steel-backed white metal shells, vary in width from 1.8in (no. 7) through 1.575in (nos 1 and 4) to 1.075in (all others). The big end journals are of 2in diameter and their shells are 1.4in wide. Forged nickel steel connecting rods carry external copper pipes to lubricate the small ends. The gudgeon pins run in floating bushes in the connecting rods, and they are held in the pistons by pads rather than circlips. Aluminium alloy pistons of a split-skirt design carry four rings, the lowest one being a scraper ring.

The camshaft is carried in seven bearings high up in the crankcase, and is driven by a set of helical gears in an aluminium casing on the front of the crankcase. The camshaft gear is made of bronze, and built in behind it is a balancer to reduce torsional vibrations in the camshaft, while the crankshaft gear incorporates its own vibration damper. Two other gears each side of the main

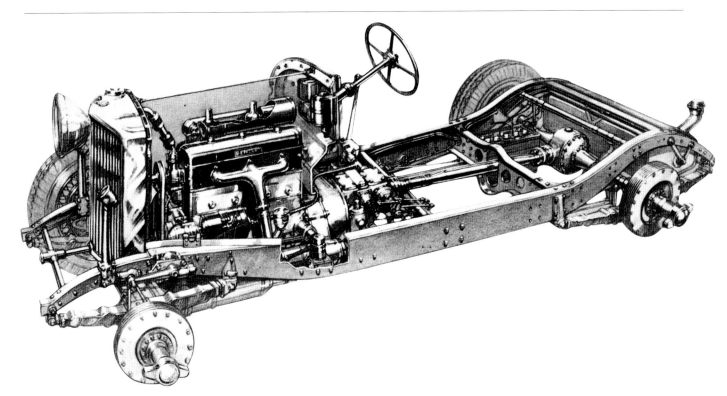

crankshaft gear wheel take auxiliary drives to the near- and offsides respectively of the engine. The offside train, driven through an idler gear, drives the distributor, oil pump and water pump, while that on the nearside is for the dynamo and also the revolution counter. Even this last drive train has its own damper, designed to eliminate oscillations in the assembly due to varying dynamo load. The oil pump, located on the outside of the engine below the distributor, takes its supply from the sump via an external pipe and strainer. Oil then passes under pressure via a main gallery to the rear of the crankshaft and thence to the main and big end journals, while separate supplies, using the over-flow from the pressure relief valve, are fed to the gear train at the front and to the rocker gear. Gravity returns take care of the camshaft bearings and cam followers.

The camshaft operates on the valves via roller cam followers, pushrods and rockers. One unusual feature of the head for its time is that it is of cross-flow design – that is, the mixture enters from one side and exhaust products are carried away on the other. Such an arrangement is recognised to give advantages in both uniformity of the petrol-air mixture and fuller scavenging of the exhaust gases. The shape of the combustion chambers is the result of extensive development, and is designed to produce the optimum amount of turbulence in the incoming mixture. The superiority of the head

design is proved by its compression ratio of 6.5:1, which was a significant advance on that of the 20/25. However the fact that the inlet and exhaust manifolds are on opposite sides of the head means that it is difficult to arrange the usual "hot spot" where the incoming mixture is preheated by the exhaust. Rolls-Royce solved the problem by arranging a feed of hot water from the cooling system to a jacket round the inlet manifold, although it involved finding a balance between warming quickly from cold and yet not over-heating the mixture in arduous conditions and causing vapour lock.

Twin horizontal SU carburettors are used – another departure, since up to that time Rolls-Royce had manufactured their own. They are mounted on a six-port manifold on the engine's offside, and are supplied with air from a large cylindrical air cleaner and silencer mounted on top of the engine. Crankcase fumes are also fed back to pass through the air cleaner. Fuel comes from an 18-gallon tank at the rear through an in-line filter to a double SU electric pump mounted on the bulkhead. The single spark plugs are fitted just below the inlet manifold, and are thus on the opposite side of the head from the valves – an arrangement which Royce had always believed led to better combustion. On the nearside of the engine the exhaust ports are siamesed into a three-branch manifold which in turn feeds an expansion

Compared with many of its contemporaries, the 3½ Litre Bentley chassis is notably light in section and lacks diagonal cross-bracing.

Two more views (upper and lower) of B89CW. Inset, for comparison, is a different dashboard treatment on an earlier chassis (B48AH).

1935 Park Ward
drophead coupé
B4CW is seen in its
original, unrestored
state. The right-hand
gear and handbrake
levers can be seen, as
can the four steering-
column controls.

Offside of the 3½ Litre engine. This is an early chassis, B12AH, which carries its spare coil on the bulkhead rather than "twinned" with the working coil.

chamber low down beside the crankcase. From there the exhaust is taken through a short silencer, then the exhaust cut-out, then to a larger silencer located in front of the rear axle.

Coolant, as we have seen, is circulated by a water pump mounted on the offside of the engine. Its temperature is controlled by radiator shutters, operated from a thermostat in the header tank. There is a fan, driven from a pulley on the front of the crankshaft, and the belt tension can be adjusted by a hand wheel. Also on the offside are the distributor, which has both centrifugal and manual timing control, and the coil. Originally there was a spare coil, together with a spare set of distributor points, mounted on the bulkhead. Later, this was changed to having the two coils mounted on the engine side by side, the second one with its own HT lead ready to be connected up. The starter motor, on the nearside, is of the pre-engaged type, which gives much quieter starting. The appearance of the engine as a whole is enhanced by a contrasting finish, the crankcase remaining in its natural aluminium while the block, head, rocker cover, carburettors and air cleaner are all finished in black enamel.

The engine, in unit with the gearbox, is mounted on two main supports, one at the front and one at the back, with steadying bearers at each side. At the front, two horizontal tubes fixed each side of the crankcase run forward to a strap suspended centrally from the chassis cross-member just behind the radiator. The rear mounting is at the back of the gearbox – originally a circular arrangement using asbestos padding, but later changed to a large rubber pad underneath. As for the sideways supports, these are tubes fixed into the rear of the crankcase which have rubber pads on their ends, and which reach as far as the chassis sides. They thus restrict oscillating movements of the engine and gearbox about their longitudinal axis, and this type of movement is further damped by friction arms at the front.

The gearbox itself, driven from a single-plate clutch of Rolls-Royce manufacture, is virtually identical to that on the Rolls-Royce 20/25hp. It has synchromesh on third and top, and second gear, while not having synchromesh, is also constant mesh (described at the time as the "silent" type). Gear ratios are understandably much closer than on the Rolls-Royce, being respectively 2.76:1,

1.73:1, 1.24:1 and 1:1. Driven off the gearbox and bolted to its nearside is the brake servo motor, which had been a feature of Rolls-Royce cars since 1924 but which was the subject of a Hispano-Suiza patent and made under licence from them. An otherwise conventional splined propellor shaft, with needle-bearing universal joints, features a damper at the front (on most but not all cars) which is intended to minimise clutch judder. The shaft drives a spiral bevel final drive and fully floating rear axle with a standard ratio of 10:41 (4.1:1). An alternative ratio of 11:43 (3.9:1) could be specified, but very few were supplied.

The brakes, assisted by the servo motor, are actuated by a combination of levers, rods and cables. Three sophisticated compensation devices in the form of miniature differential gears equalise the effort from side to side, for the front, rear and hand brakes respectively. Compensation between front and rear is an integral part of the servo mechanism's operation. The handbrake operates on a separate set of shoes in the rear drums. At the front the final connection is via levers which pivot on rods set within the axle beam itself. Two extra features have been added to minimise any fierceness from the servo action: a friction damper to avoid the brakes grabbing when first applied, and a vacuum damper to counter the opposite effect when the brakes are released.

A cast aluminium bulkhead separates the engine compartment from the driver. Both the gear lever and the handbrake lever are located to the right of the driver's seat, in pursuit of the company's long-held view that the driver should be able to leave the car from the nearside door if necessary. Around the boss of the four-spoke wheel are levers for hand throttle, mixture, ignition timing and headlamp dipping, while in the centre is the button controlling the twin horns. The standard instrument layout supplied with the car places them in two groups. In the centre of the dashboard, in an oval panel, are an ammeter and gauges for petrol, water temperature and oil pressure. In the middle of these gauges is a combined switch and key lock for ignition and lights, and there are also an ignition warning light and a switch for instrument lighting. On the right of the dashboard, in front of the driver, is a second oval panel which houses two larger instruments – a speedometer and a combined revolution counter and clock. The starter button and windscreen wiper knob are also on the dash, as are a cigarette lighter and an ashtray. Under the dash can be found the tap for the two-gallon reserve petrol supply and also the lever operating the centralised chassis lubrication system, the reservoir for which is located on the scuttle.

This, therefore, was the car which was revealed to the press, sales agents and favoured customers at the end of September 1933, priced at £1100. No-one actually saw the chassis, except Gordon Crosby of *The Autocar* who had been allowed into Park Ward's premises to sketch one ready for the magazine's announcement issue of 6 October. In return for this privilege, Crosby was asked to "make his drawing look not too much like a Rolls-

Braking layout, showing the action of the servo unit. Each pair of brakes - footbrake front and rear, and handbrake - has its own gear-type equaliser.

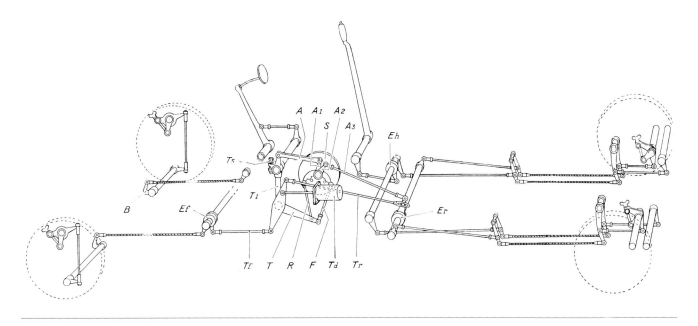

Here and on the facing page is a James Young two-seat drophead coupé on 1934 chassis B52CR. There is a separate locker for golf-clubs - note the second small door on the nearside.

Park Ward's standard drophead coupé is shown here on chassis B15CW of January 1935.

This is the later type of standard Park Ward saloon with a larger luggage boot.

Royce by featuring those parts that are different and dealing lightly with those parts that are the same". The magazine was also allowed a drive in the car in time to publish some impressions in the same issue, and from the illustrations it is clear that they used the prototype open car with Park Ward bodywork. *The Motor* were less favoured: not only did they not obtain a test drive but they also appear to have been given out-of-date information from which to write their description (it referred both to coolant temperature control by thermostat and to a mechanical fuel pump).

The cars which appeared at the press luncheon at the Royal Ascot Hotel were of three different body types. The four-door saloon and drophead coupé styles were of course by Park Ward, but the Park Ward open four-seater had disappeared and was replaced by a new design from Vanden Plas. This latter was now to be the standard open bodywork on offer, and it differed markedly in appearance from its Park Ward predecessor in having valanced wings and a longer bonnet. The

journalists were not allowed to drive the cars, but were offered rides round the local roads. WO Bentley was present at this event, and recounts in his autobiography how he settled a long-standing score with the hotel owner, who had failed to recognise him. "I invited him to come round [the test course] with me in the front seat on the last lap of the day, when the brakes were feeling a little tired. By then my eye was well in and I felt I knew the road and the car thoroughly. I had him holding

on like grim death before I skidded to a halt in front of his hotel again, and told him who I was."

In this way Rolls-Royce were able to control quite carefully the write-ups which then appeared about the new car. In any case it was not the done thing in those days to be openly critical, especially when your host had just bought you a good lunch. The motoring correspondents of the daily press concentrated on descriptions of the car's ride and roadholding, which were obviously gleaned from

A fine example of the Owen sedanca coupé design, numerous examples of which were built by Gurney Nutting. This is on a 1934 chassis, B55BL.

Thrupp & Maberly developed their own standard design of four-door, four-light saloon. It is shown here on chassis B189BL (September 1934).

their time as passengers at Ascot. This was the fate of *The Motor* and *Motor Sport* as well, but of course these publications added much fuller technical descriptions of the car, together with a reminder of the recent history of the Bentley marque. All agreed that, as *The Autocar* put it, "a car of the Bentley type manufactured with the organisation Rolls-Royce possess seemed likely to be something altogether out of the common". *The Motor* added, rather plaintively, that "at the time of writing it has not proved possible to obtain photographs or technical drawings of the new chassis, as these are in process of having coachwork fitted for exhibition at Olympia". What they thought when their rival appeared three days later with a full chassis drawing can only be imagined

Thus it was left to Geoffrey Smith, managing editor of *The Autocar*, to be the first to write about what it was like to drive one of these cars. The photographs illustrating his article show him in the fourth experimental car 4-B-IV, registration RC1351, which of course was the one fitted with the Park Ward tourer body. The particular points which he warmed to were to be familiar ones in ensuing months – the flexibility of the engine, fierce acceleration when wanted, "remarkable" roadholding, "exceptional" servo brakes, "a springing system which is remarkably effective in conjunction with hydraulic shock absorbers", and yet all achieved in comparative silence. Smith correctly pinpointed low weight as being the key

to the car's acceleration, and seemed delighted with its overall performance, achieving an indicated maximum of 93mph on his trip round the roads of Hertfordshire.

Although the phrase "standardised coachwork" was not encouraged, one can detect that the company was making sure that certain designs were being given maximum publicity. These were two (initially three) from Park Ward and one from Vanden Plas, and they corresponded to the demonstration cars made available at the launch. Park Ward – virtually an in-house operation for Rolls-Royce, since they held a minority stake in the business – would be pleased to provide the four-door sports saloon, priced at £1460, or the drophead coupé at £1485. The same coachbuilder initially offered a two-door saloon as well, but the much higher price of £1635 seems to have led to this design being dropped from the line-up. Vanden Plas had replaced Park Ward as suppliers of the open four-seat tourer, which was priced at £1380. Other coachbuilders had obviously been sent chassis drawings in advance, since the launch publicity included details of designs from Barker, Freestone & Webb, Gurney Nutting, Hooper, H J Mulliner and Thrupp & Maberly. A Bentley London showroom was now open next to the Rolls-Royce one in Conduit Street, and top dealers such as Jack Barclay and H R Owen were ready to take orders.

The balance between the motoring magazines was redressed later in October when both *The*

Motor and *Motor Sport* were offered a car for extended test. This was B1AE, registered ALU321, the first production chassis and the first to be given a Vanden Plas body. *The Motor*'s journalists were obviously enthralled by the car, and understandably at this level of quality could find very little to criticise. More than that, it fell into a previously unknown category, one which combined sports car performance with great refinement. "The 3½ Litre Bentley gives a performance which would satisfy the most exacting critic, and, at the same time, is a car of exceptional comfort, refinement and attractive individuality". Confidence and control were other qualities to impress them. "Even when the Bentley is driven up to the limits of speed on the gears, or if thrown round corners and braked violently, the performance remains refined, for every control fulfils its functions smoothly, progressively and consistently in a way which inspires complete confidence." As well as performance, though, there were the usual compliments for roadholding and ride. The testers measured a maximum speed of 91mph (with the windscreen folded) and an acceleration time from 0-60mph of 18 seconds. Their one minor quibble was with the brakes, which tended to lock the rear wheels somewhat early, but this was a deliberate feature of the servo system intended to ensure that the driver could steer at all times.

The summation of *The Motor* was that the Bentley was "a car for long journeys and high average speeds, for unobtrusive performance, for majestic pottering, for crowded roads; in fact, for interpreting every whim of the driver in an effortless way". The testers from *Motor Sport* would have agreed totally. They put the same car through its paces and came up with very similar conclusions – even down to the measured maximum speed of 91mph. Their only minor quibble was with the brakes, where it appeared that washing had sprayed water into one of the drums. Silence was a quality which particularly impressed them, the exhaust note being described as "almost inaudible". They attributed the "surprising" performance, correctly, to a combination of engine power (quoted at 120bhp though the actual figure was 114), moderate chassis weight and "the small frontal area made possible by the double-dropped frame". They were rather further from the mark, however, when they tried to analyse the suspension characteristics. "The suspension is good over the car's entire speed range. Going slowly over a rough surface, one does not get those jabs associated with a fast car with tight 'shockers', yet at 85mph there is no swinging or rolling at corners. This must be due largely to correct weight distribution and a stiff chassis, for on the majority of cars fitted only with hydraulic shock-absorbers a certain amount of movement takes place before the steadying effect is felt". As far as the chassis went they could hardly have been more wrong, since – as we shall see – it was one of the least rigid

H J Mulliner were another high-class coachbuilder who produced a standard design of sports saloon for the Bentley. This is chassis B78BN.

A 1935 Thrupp & Maberly drophead coupé on chassis B200DG, with the high boot line characteristic of this coachbuilder. Wheel discs were a common accessory at the time.
Opposite: *A different type of H J Mulliner saloon, this time a two-door. This very early chassis (B66AH) has had an additional bracing tube fitted across the headlamp supports.*

B34CR

Another example of an Owen sedanca coupé (built for London dealer Capt H R Owen). Barker gained the first order, but thereafter the business - including this chassis, B34CR - went to Gurney Nutting.

amongst the chassis introduced that year. What these highly experienced testers had failed to realise was just how good the Rolls-Royce shock absorbers were – and that was before the speed-related or driver-controlled features had been added to the Bentley.

Motor Sport, understandably, were keen to make comparisons with the old 4½ Litre Bentley. They found that the new car was much lower and was four inches shorter in the wheelbase, but that passengers, although sitting closer together, were all carried within the wheelbase. A more pertinent comparison was with the 20/25hp Rolls-Royce, where WO Bentley himself faithfully carried out instructions by pointing out how different it was in nearly every particular (only the sump is common to the two engines, and so on). The company at this stage was still nervous about the impact of the

Bentley on sales of the smaller Rolls-Royce, although on the other hand it was only too pleased to claim Rolls-Royce standards of design and crafts-manship for the new car.

Meanwhile the 1933 Olympia Show had opened, and Bentleys were to be found every-where. The company had taken a separate stand for the new marque, and on it were a Vanden Plas four-seat tourer, a Park Ward four-door saloon and a Park Ward drophead coupé. Interestingly, there was no stripped chassis on show, something which might have been expected with a new model. However these exhibits were only the beginning, as the coachbuilding section of the show was full of Bentleys. Barker were showing a three-position drophead coupé, which later became their demon-strator for a year, while Hooper's stand had another version of the four-door sports saloon

In March 1934 Thrupp & Maberly built this streamlined fixed-head coupé on chassis B67AE for Geoffrey Smith, editorial director of The Autocar.

style. The Arthur Mulliner stand also contained a four-door sports saloon, but it must have arrived late as *The Autocar*'s reporter made no mention of the car.

H J Mulliner's exhibit was the first example of the "Owen sedanca coupé", so called because it was commissioned by the West End dealer Capt H R Owen. This was a particularly neat example of a three-position drophead coupé, with an apparently separate trunk at the back in the "Continental" manner rather than a built-in luggage boot. It proved to be a one-off, as thereafter Owen took his business to Gurney Nutting. Despite it not being mentioned in the catalogue, Park Ward apparently decided to show their two-door sports saloon (chassis B23AE); this later became an experimental car and was used for streamlining tests. On the Rippon stand could be seen yet another four-door

sports saloon, while Thrupp & Maberly had an example of their three-position drophead coupé; this car became a Jack Barclay demonstrator for a time. Vanden Plas, somewhat surprisingly, did not feature a Bentley on their own stand, presumably because their four-seat tourer was already being displayed by the manufacturers themselves. (Full details of all the exhibits including chassis numbers are listed in Appendix 1)

By the time the Motor Show was over Rolls-Royce must have felt that the launch of the new Bentley could hardly have gone better. It was clear that there was still a great deal of goodwill towards the Bentley name, and no-one had suggested that the new model was anything other than a worthy replacement for the much loved green cars. The company had withheld sufficient technical details to prevent the technical press realising exactly how

Barker sedanca coupé on chassis B33AE, delivered to Capt J F C Kruse in February 1934. This was one of the first two deliveries to private customers.

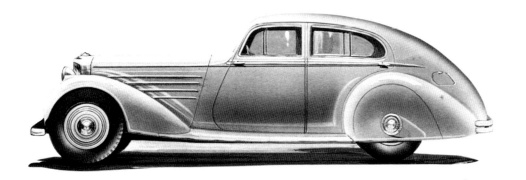

Thrupp & Maberly developed their ideas further for the 1934 Olympia Show, on chassis B30BN. It bristled with features which would come to typify late 1930s styling.

*Further views of
B200DG, showing
the three-position
hood in use. A spare
wheel recessed and
covered in the boot
lid was another
common Thrupp &
Maberly feature at
this period.*

An impressive frontal view of B200DG. Both the trumpet horns and the mascot are likely to have been later additions - especially since the official Bentley mascot was not on sale until the following year.

E R Hall's special-bodied and highly tuned 3½ Litre Bentley taking part in the 1934 Tourist Trophy.

much the 20/25 and the new car had in common, and had thus sidestepped any direct comparison with – and possibly sales impact on – the smaller Rolls-Royce. It had even presented the two years' delay in launching the car as merely what was required for proper development, rather than what it really was – dithering followed by an unseemly scramble.

Such rosy thoughts would have been rudely interrupted by the arrival of the 21 November issue of *The Automobile Engineer*, incidentally a sister publication of *The Autocar*. That particular issue each year traditionally contained a full analysis of the Motor Show exhibits under various headings, and the Bentley came in for some forceful criticism under several of them. One article, titled "Frames: Universal Adoption of Diagonal Cross-bracing", propounded that "diagonal cross-bracing has been found to contribute so largely to road-holding qualities, body silence and the like, that it is now practically universal". Later, therefore, it was forced to examine the Bentley's refusal to join this universal trend. "In the new Bentley chassis every attempt has obviously been made to reduce weight as far as possible. It is a pity, however, that the frame of the car should have been chosen as one of the principal subjects of this weight reduction. It

is six [sic] inches deep, has one good tubular cross-member behind the gear box, but no other cross-members of any appreciable torsional stiffness. It is, moreover, only ⅛ inches thick. While the car is, of course, much lighter than the old Bentleys, a better foundation would have been an advantage."

The magazine had touched on the one great mystery of the car's success. One would have thought that an essentially vintage design, using a rather flimsy, flexible chassis with non-independent leaf springs all round, would have behaved on the road like any other vintage design – that is, with a hard ride on anything but smooth roads, and a low limit of adhesion on corners. Instead, the Experimental department had pulled a rabbit out of the hat, and had cobbled together a vehicle which showed most of its contemporaries how a car should behave. What was the secret? If it was neither the chassis nor the springs, then it must surely be the damping. When *Motor Sport* attributed the car's excellent road manners to a stiff chassis, what they were really doing, unwittingly, was paying a massive compliment to the dampers – or rather to the damping, if we remind ourselves of the trouble the company took to eliminate inter-leaf friction in the springs.

Automobile Engineer had not finished: they also had rather a low opinion of the Bentley's engine. After describing its carburation as "quite conventional", they then waded into the manifolding. "The [carburettor] intake [is] surrounded by a surprisingly small water jacket, which is fed from the cylinder head and exhausted by a lead taken to the suction side of the pump in the normal manner. Warming up is likely to be a rather lengthy process, and it is rather surprising that in this age water jacketing should still be employed. Quicker warming up could, of course, have been obtained with a suitable type of hot spot " They then go on to recognise that this is more difficult with a cross-flow head but nevertheless propose a workable scheme. Their points are valid as far as they go, and indeed Hives had argued during the development process against a water-heating scheme for precisely these reasons.

Finally, *Automobile Engineer* were also dissatisfied with the brakes; not with the braking, it must be said, since no road test was involved, but with the basic design. Their particular problem concerned the small diameter of the brake drums – smaller, they pointed out, than the Aston Martin

which had an engine of less than half the Bentley's capacity. They were honest enough to accept that the actual performance of the brakes was likely to be satisfactory given that they were servo assisted. Nevertheless the writers felt that a buyer of a car in this class expected large diameter brake drums, and they saw no reason why he shouldn't be given them!

It was all to the good, from the company's point of view, that this carping took place in a fairly highbrow technical journal rather than in, say, the daily press. It had no perceptible impact on the way in which the car was received, and the orders started flowing in. Inevitably there was something of a pause while chassis started arriving at the coachbuilders and customers waited impatiently for their cars to be completed. One suspects, however, that the delay was extended a little so that the Experimental department could complete their testing programme. Advertising for the new car had begun in October, but it was given fresh impetus by a stroke of genius. In early 1934 an old slogan, "The Silent Sports Car", made a reappearance. It had first been used in 1928, but it was to become forever associated with the post-1931

An incident in the 1935 TT, captured by artist Gordon Crosby, when Von der Becke's Riley went into the sandbank as Eddie Hall sailed by.

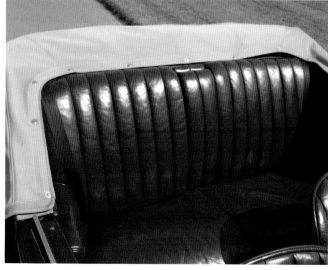

Interior views of B200DG, the Thrupp & Maberly drophead coupé. Back seat width is adequate, although necessarily restricted by the folded hood. The driver's seat, meanwhile, has all the adjustment one might need.

Bentley. The phrase so encapsulated the public's feelings about the new Bentley that it immediately went into the language, and thus became a priceless advertising property. From then on, if anyone mentioned the name Bentley (or very often "Rolls Bentley") the "Silent Sports Car" would hover subconsciously in the mind.

There then followed a rather childish competition for the title of first owner of one of the new cars. Two different buyers claimed the honour during February 1934 – Capt Kruse with his Barker sedanca coupé and Mr R F Summers who had taken delivery of a Park Ward saloon. Eventually the company had to solve the argument by declaring a dead heat. A more useful form of competition occurred in March, when the RAC Bournemouth Rally attracted an interesting entry in the coachwork section. This was a period of intense interest in streamlining, when coachbuilders vied with each other to produce cars with sloping tails and (later) curved frontal treatments. Park Ward produced what we would now call a fastback body on chassis B41AE, registered AMV424, and it won not only its class but also the premier award for two-door closed cars. A sports saloon, the car bore a resemblance to an experimental body which Evernden had designed on chassis B23AE, and which the Experimental department were using for wind-resistance tests at Brooklands. The Bournemouth Rally car had

Engine compartment of B200DG. The extra tappings from the cooling system are for a heater which has been added at some time in its life. The large black cylinder on the nearside bulkhead is the reservoir for the chassis lubrication system.

deeply valanced wings with no running boards, and its extended tail enclosed both the spare wheel and substantial luggage capacity.

Thrupp & Maberly were another coachbuilder to try out a streamlined design on a Bentley chassis. Their client was none other than Geoffrey Smith, director of the Iliffe publishing group and managing editor of *The Autocar*, whom we last met testing the prototype Park Ward tourer. A full description of the project, on chassis B67AE (registered AXO1), appeared in the magazine in May 1934. It was an early essay in the style which became known as "two-door pillarless", as there was no central pillar to support the upper half of each door, the door and quarter glasses merely overlapping. It differed from the Park Ward RAC Rally entry in having running boards, but resembled it in its large boot, which it was claimed would swallow five large suitcases. Later that year Thrupp & Maberly developed their streamlining ideas further on another Bentley, and attracted much attention at the Olympia Show as a result. Their sloping-tail, four-door saloon on chassis B30BN had vestigial running boards, virtually no separate rear wings, and the rear wheels covered in with spats.

In his article, Smith commented perceptively that "at the moment, in this country, the preference seems to be for a streamlined body only, the front of the car presenting an orthodox appearance". In a follow-up article after he had covered some 10,000 miles in the car, he realistically rated its advantages as primarily increased luggage space, second modern appearance, thirdly its ability to remain clean (because of improved airflow) and only fourth the supposed major benefits of streamlining – namely speed and economy. Without having conducted measured tests, his impression was that the car's maximum was a few mph higher than the standard body, and that economy was around 20mpg as opposed to 18. The implication was that limited streamlining in this form produced modest benefits, but that major advances would only come about when the conventional bluff front and vertical radiator could be altered. Back at Derby, Hives and Robotham were coming to the same conclusion.

It was not until May that *The Autocar* managed to put the Bentley through a full road test, using a standard Park Ward four-door saloon. Commenting that it represented both the modern idea of a high performance car and yet also a car that could be quiet and docile in traffic, they decided that "dual character" was the expression that best summed the car up. They achieved a two-way average maximum speed of 92mph with a best one-way figure of 94mph. Acceleration from 0 to 60mph took 20.4 seconds, which was some way off *The Motor's* time of 18 seconds in the Vanden Plas tourer. One might think that this was a matter of either gearing or weight, but the figures belie this;

A Park Ward "streamline saloon", thought to be chassis B82BN which was Park Ward's 1934 Olympia Show car, finished in coronet red with black moulding.

both cars had the 4.1:1 rear axle, and the stated weights were 30cwt (1525kg) for the saloon and 29½cwt (1500kg) for the tourer. The testers were particularly impressed with the car's handling. "It is a matter of very considerable difficulty to design springing which will be both comfortable at ordinary speeds for all the occupants of the car and at the same time allow it to be driven safely – a point which implies stability of a high order – at speeds in the region of 90 mph. It can be said that most definitely an excellent compromise between these two separate, widely divergent needs has been achieved."

Park Ward's standard saloon coachwork itself

was the subject of a detailed analysis some months later at the hands of "Tenon", specialist coachwork writer for *The Motor*. Not always an easy person to please, Tenon was noticeably complimentary about this body, and gave special praise to the space in the rear seats. "The unusually long footwells help in this, for the tallest man can settle right down into the back seat without knee-restriction." However the compliment should really be reserved for Rolls-Royce rather than Park Ward, as it was they who had exploited the use of footwells during the development of the car. They admired the way in which the Riley company used footwells; a memo from Day at the time read in

Another Park Ward streamline saloon, similar to B82BN but with a longer tail. This is chassis B86CR dating from July 1935.

Gurney Nutting produced this "pillarless coupé" on chassis B4BN, finished in marooon, for their 1934 Olympia Show stand.

William Arnold of Manchester developed their "Slipstream" design of saloon, seen here applied to chassis B129DK in 1935.

part: "The Riley Monaco saloon is a magnificent example of how to make the best use of a given body space when the latter is small. As the result of borrowing one of these cars we learnt a great deal, and have subsequently found it necessary to entirely revise our Bensport layouts".

Although Rolls-Royce had set its face against

ever being involved in racing, with its reputation for uncontrollable costs, they were persuaded to make an exception for the 1934 Ulster Tourist Trophy race. Their valued customer E R (Eddie) Hall proposed to enter his 3½ Litre car, and wondered if the company might help. This suggestion found favour, not least because the company

Kellner of Paris built this fixed head coupé on chassis B73EJ in late 1935.

was involved in a programme both to increase the power of the engine and to try out improved bearing materials. It could maintain the overt position that Hall's was a totally private entry, while in the background giving him assistance to obtain a good result. The potential benefits for Rolls-Royce were publicity for the marque and a useful boost

to their test programme.

Hall had used his car, chassis B35AE, to practice for the Mille Miglia, and it needed considerable work to make it ready for the TT. Not least was to change the original Abbott tourer body for one which conformed with the regulations but which would be of maximum benefit in the race. This task

Also a 1934 Show car, this is an Arthur Mulliner sports saloon on chassis B183BL, originally finished in light blue and silver.

The Swiss coachbuilder Graber built two bodies on 3½ Litre chassis. This one is thought to be chassis B149BL, delivered July 1934.

An unusual sports saloon in pillarless style from Bertelli, on chassis B58DG (July 1935).

Thrupp & Maberly supplied this drophead coupé on chassis B110DG for Geoffrey Smith of The Autocar *in April 1935 – only a year after his streamlined saloon from the same coachbuilder.*

was given to the coachbuilders Offord, who produced a lightweight body, nominally a four-seater, of advanced construction. Aluminium panels covered a duralumin framework, the seat frames were made of elektron, and a streamlined fairing over the rear of the car directed cooling air to the brakes. At the same time the factory increased the engine power to 131bhp by various means, including raising the compression ratio to 7.75:1 and fitting larger inlet valves. The big end bearings were changed to lead bronze, since the company knew that the standard white-metal bearings on the 3½ Litre would be at risk of breaking down at higher loads, and they were already using lead bronze on their aero engines. Other modifications included additional friction shock absorbers, a higher rear axle ratio (3.75:1) and a 26-gallon petrol tank.

In the race Hall managed to come a highly creditable second, being beaten on handicap but managing to finish ahead of the Lagonda team of 4½-litre cars. He also posted the highest average race speed at 78.4mph. Indeed but for an unfortunate delay during a tyre change, when a wheel nut seized, he might well have won. He entered the same car in the 1935 race. The engine now had a compression ratio of 8.35:1 and a totally revised induction system, and produced 152bhp. He also fitted a different design of wing in an attempt

to reduce air resistance, although the effect of this change on lap speed was later shown to be negligible. Once again he was second on handicap, and again he put up the fastest average at 80.4mph. These results showed convincingly that the new Bentley was one of the fastest cars on the market, and did much to temper mutterings about it being a "promenade car".

Another racing driver who was a prolific user and consumer of Bentleys was Raymond Mays of ERA fame. In his case the cars were used primarily for transport around Europe from race to race, although one performed sterling service when Mays used it for a week's unofficial practice on the Nurburgring. In all Mays got through five cars in the period 1935-39 – one 3½ Litre, two 4¼ Litres and one "overdrive" model owned personally, and one 4¼ Litre loaned to him by the company for travel between races during the 1937-8 South African season. In this last car he "accidentally" set up a new unofficial record for the trip from East London to Cape Town. It goes without saying that Mays was a fervent admirer of the car. Whether, as one rumour has it, he was influenced by the very favourable price he paid for his cars is another matter.

By the time the Olympia Show came round again in 1934, the Bentley was the chassis of

The Kellner coupé B73EJ has benefited from a ground-up restoration. It was an advanced design for its time, for example in the way it dispensed with running-boards. Additional high-intensity horns have been added under the bonnet. Knurled nuts holding the valve chest covers are one means of distinguishing the 3½-litre engine from its 4¼-litre successor.

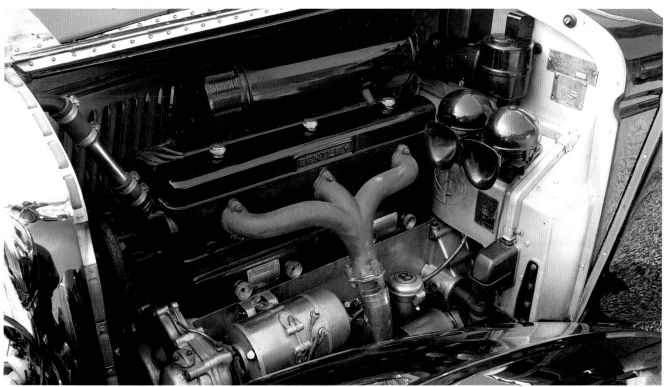

A smart two-tone treatment on chassis B120DG, a standard Park Ward four-door saloon from April 1935.

James Young called this design a "sedanca coupé" when they built it on chassis B184DG in June 1935, but we would know it as a three-position drophead coupé.

choice for any coachbuilder worthy of the name. As well as the three standard body styles shown on the company's own stand, no less than 14 coach-building firms exhibited their work on the Bentley chassis. Streamlining was still very much in vogue, and as well as the dramatic Thrupp & Maberly four-door saloon mentioned previously (labelled "Aerodynamic") there was a streamline saloon from Park Ward and a "Slipstream" saloon from William Arnold, the Manchester coachbuilder. Most of the remainder were the ubiquitous four-door four-light saloons, but there was a sprinkling of coupés, drophead and other. (Full details of all the exhibits including chassis numbers are listed in Appendix 1)

From the outset, modifications to the chassis specification had been introduced as soon as they were approved. The first, from the 16th car onwards (B33AE), involved the radiator mounting, where the previous rigid arrangement was changed to a "centre point" system allowing it a small amount of lateral movement. Another comparatively early change was to the engine lubrication system, where leaks had been found to occur in the copper pipes carrying oil up the connecting rods. Instead the rods were bored internally, and at the same time the opportunity was taken to make a drilling through the rod to allow spray lubrication of the cylinder wall. Other changes during the two-year life of the 3½ Litre model covered such things as pressed-in small end bushes instead of floating, a lightened flywheel,

the addition of a propellor shaft damper, a geared starter drive, water excluders on the front brakes and the adoption of Lucas P100 headlamps.

There were also a series of modifications aimed at curing the tendency of the front of the car to shake badly. In fact the altered radiator mounting mentioned above comes under this heading, since it was intended to disconnect the radiator from any shaking of the wings and headlamps. (This problem was so bad on certain cars that one owner had to have two sets of replacement front wings in eight months.) Also, of course, the two chassis frame changes mentioned earlier – replacing the front chassis cross tube with a much more substantial component, albeit dropped so that it was concealed by the apron, and adding further strengthening below the headlamp supports – were designed to make the front of the chassis more rigid. In addition to this strengthening, it was decided to fit the Wilmot-Breeden stabilising front bumper as standard, and this item was fitted retrospectively to a number of cars where front end shake had been a particular problem.

There was even some discussion about boxing in the front chassis members, based on the company's experience with an imported Essex Terraplane. That car, incidentally, was also responsible for the change to a rubber gearbox mounting, since the rubber engine mountings on the Essex had been a revelation to the Derby management. This was only a palliative, however, and there was general agreement that what was really required was a much stronger chassis. Ideally (Elliott

admitted, in July 1934) this should be diagonally braced in the centre, but this in turn would require the gearbox to be mounted independently of the engine. Then the engine could be mounted much more flexibly – a total reversal of the car's Peregrine origins, which assumed that the rigidly mounted engine would add strength to the chassis.

Another very significant improvement to the car's specification was to the hydraulic dampers. On the Phantom II and 20/25 Rolls-Royce had introduced a sophisticated control for the damping system, whereby its characteristics could be varied according to both the speed of the car and the requirements of the driver. Given that the Bentley used the same dampers as the two Rolls-Royce models, its adoption was inevitable, and this happened at the beginning of 1935. A pump mounted on the offside of the gearbox pumps oil to the shock absorbers (this pump, described as a "jewel" by one expert restorer, is an expensive piece of precision engineering). At the shock absorber the fluid acts on a bellows which in turn is connected to the spring controlling the bypass valves. Thus the fluid pressure controls the stiffness of the shock absorbers, and as the car's speed rises and the pump pressure increases, the shock absorbers are automatically stiffened. The sophistication is taken further, in that the pump produces differential pressures for the front and rear pairs. As an added refinement, the pressure of the fluid at any given speed can be altered manually by controlling a bypass valve. This control is in the hands of the driver, and takes the form of a lever on

A noticeably more conservative design than their 1934 Show car, Thrupp & Maberly described this sports saloon as "semi-streamline" when they built it on chassis B1DK in June 1935.

Lancefield's version of the streamline saloon, on chassis B159DK in September 1935, shows advanced features such as minimal running boards and pontoon-style wings.

the steering wheel boss. To accommodate this new control, the former dipswitch lever is deleted and instead there is a foot-operated dipswitch on the floor.

The Motor tried the system out immediately, and were impressed. "With the lever in the minimum position the damping action is reduced to a setting which is admirably suited to moderate speeds on rough roads", whereas "the new control is of value [at speed], as an increase in damping reduces front-axle movements and so steadies the steering effectively for fast cruising." The testers were particularly struck by the system's speed of response: "...in consequence, a change in damping

can be effected as speedily as alterations in road surface are encountered on a fast car". Neverthe-less they also emphasised the other benefit of the system: "an automatic increase in the damping as the speed rises, which occurs irrespective of the location of the hand control.". Thus the Bentley was able to keep ahead of advances which other marques were making by, for example, adopting the André Telecontrol system.

On a more frivolous note, the company was still struggling to find a suitable mascot, which owners were apparently demanding. In February 1935, announcing a public competition to find a suitable design, the company confessed that it was "not

This saloon by Mayfair, on chassis B177DK (June 1935), shows typical Mayfair features such as faired-in sidelamps.

quite satisfied with the present mascot", which in its illustration appeared to be the Sykes design mentioned in the previous chapter. Presumably this item was available on request, although it has to be said that most of the cars up to that time seem to have elected not to have a mascot. A prize of £50 – a substantial sum in those days – would go to the winner, and entries of either birds or the female form were barred. Even this extreme step did not get the company out of its difficulty, as in December of that year it announced that none of the entries was satisfactory, awarding two £25 consolation prizes instead. However it soon settled on a new design of its own, and mascots began to appear on Bentley radiators.

At the 1935 Olympia Show the Bentley was even more in evidence than before, with a total of 20 chassis including the usual three on the company's own stand. While a number of designs still showed the influence of the streamline movement, the most influential newcomer was without doubt to be found on Freestone & Webb's stand. There, under the description "brougham saloon", was a closed car with unusual sculpted edges along its roof and sides. This was the car which effectively started the "razor edge" style, echoes of

which continued right through to the 1960s. Park Ward showed a coupé de ville on chassis B135EJ; there was more to this car than met the eye, as we shall see. (Full details of all the exhibits including chassis numbers are listed in Appendix 1)

Towards the end of the year *The Motor* decided to put the Bentley through another test. This time their choice fell on the Park Ward drophead coupé, and the usual compliments came tumbling out – silence, refinement, response to controls, ability to perform fast journeys and so on. The car had the new controllable shock absorbers, but the fact that they attracted no special comment was probably a compliment in that they must have functioned unobtrusively. The testers achieved a satisfactory maximum speed of 90mph, but for once omitted an acceleration time from 0 to 60mph. Their 0-50mph time was 12.8 seconds, which compares with 13.4 seconds when *The Autocar* tested the Park Ward saloon 18 months previously. Since the drophead's weight was a hefty 32½cwt (1635kg) one suspects that there had been some development work on the engine over that period.

By the end of 1935, less than two years after deliveries of the new Bentley had started in earnest, the success of the car was assured. Sales

In October 1935 Freestone & Webb (under their "Freestone Endura" name) built an early version of the concealed-head style coupé, on chassis B94EF.

Windover built this rather Art Deco drophead coupé on chassis B91EJ for the 1935 Paris Salon, but credit for the design goes to Vanden Plas.

had reached the 1000 mark, which for a car costing £1380 upwards was a magnificent achievement. Moreover there was no indication that sales of the smaller Rolls-Royce had been affected. The "Silent Sports Car" had found its own place in the market, outperforming its presumed rivals such as the Alvis Speed Twenty and the M45 Lagonda. Furthermore it had shown that it could hold its head up in terms of performance on the road even though its specification (damping system apart) was in many ways less advanced. The Alvis, for example, which had often been the standard by which the Experimental department had judged its own cars, by 1933 had both independent front suspension and synchromesh on all four gears. Bearing in mind that its engine capacity was only 2½ Litres, its performance was near but not quite up to that of the Bentley; its maximum speed was just under 90mph rather than just over, and its acceleration times were slightly inferior.

The Lagonda M45, also launched in time for the 1933 Show, was another matter. Importantly, it had the advantage of a significantly larger engine at 4½ Litres, which gave it the edge on performance. The tourer would reach 60mph from rest in 15.4 seconds and had a maximum speed of 93.7mph, the corresponding figures for the saloon being 15.8 seconds and 90.0mph. The car was well made, and the body styles available from the factory were attractive. On the other hand it was no more

advanced technically than the Bentley, and with its crash gearbox it was at a positive disadvantage. However the arrival in 1935 of the more powerful Rapide version must have made Rolls-Royce sit up and take notice, especially when *The Autocar* testers produced a 0-60mph acceleration time of 14.6 seconds and a mean maximum speed of 98.4mph. Even the question of sporting heritage was swinging Lagonda's way when they announced a team entry for the 1935 Le Mans, and doubly so when the cars went on to win. It was ironic that virtually at that same moment the company called in the receivers and the shine went off their reputation. Rolls-Royce promptly tried to buy the company, presumably with termination in mind, but were outbid by London solicitor Alan Good. His first act was to persuade WO Bentley to leave Rolls-Royce and work for him instead. By the end of 1935 Lagonda had reinstated themselves as the Bentley marque's greatest threat.

Comparisons of these competitors' performance and technical specifications, however, important though they may be, are of less significance than the question of price. The Lagonda and the Alvis, although very similar to the Bentley as we have seen, were substantially lower in price – dramatically so in the case of the Alvis. If one compares the standard four-door saloons of the three models, the Alvis was £850, Lagonda £950, and Bentley £1460. It was the same with the tourer models – Alvis £700, Lagonda £825, Bentley £1380. By all normal yardsticks it should have been Bentley calling in the receivers, yet Bentley sales equalled those of the two other marques combined, as far as one can tell from the records available. How the company achieved this Indian rope trick is one of the great marketing mysteries of the 1930s.

The most likely explanation is that, in spite of the company's efforts to the contrary, the Bentley was imbued in the minds of its customers with all the values of a Rolls-Royce – it was a Rolls-Bentley, no matter what it said on the radiator. Such a car would never attract the deerstalker brigade, who under no circumstances would regard the new Bentley as a proper sports car, but it spoke volumes to those who appreciated comfort as well as performance. For these people, given that they could afford it, the extra appeal of something made by Rolls-Royce made all the difference. They could never see themselves in a Rolls-Royce – that would send out quite the wrong message to their friends – so there was no question of the Bentley biting into sales of the 20/25, even though its price was very similar.

In marketing terms, the Bentley had overnight become the ultimate aspirational car. If you could afford it, you bought it; if you couldn't, you bought something else – maybe a Lagonda, maybe an Alvis, possibly a Talbot or a Railton – but you still aspired to a Bentley next time. It had achieved this position virtually by chance, while its makers

This is almost certainly B125EJ, Freestone & Webb's 1935 Olympia Show car and the one with which they began the craze for "razor-edge" styling. It was finished in birch grey with red upholstery.

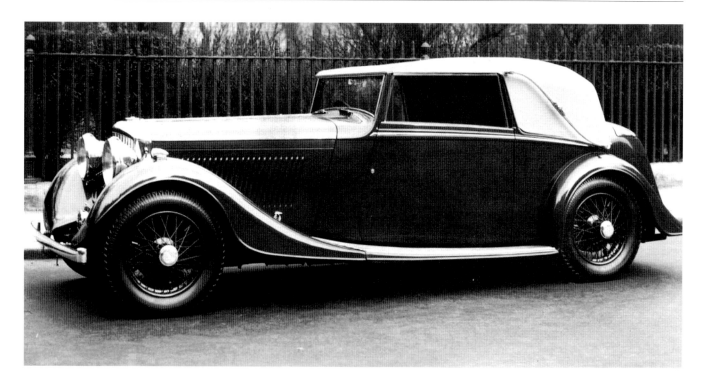

Another Thrupp & Maberly drophead coupé, on chassis B109FC of February 1936. Compared with B110DG on page 67 it has lost its wing-mounted spare wheel, which is now presumably in the tail.

By early 1936, when they built this "pillarless saloon coupé" on chassis B196FB, Gurney Nutting were showing much more confidence in the style (compare it with B4BN on page 63).

wrung their hands and wished it could have been totally different – smaller, cheaper, supercharged, anything. Yet in spite of themselves Rolls-Royce had found a new market segment, and theirs was the only car in it.

Back at Derby, while they were glad of the business, there were concerns at the direction in which their creation was heading. In particular its reliance on light weight for its good performance was being imperilled by the efforts of the coachbuilders. Whereas the expectation had been that it would be perceived as a sports car, with perhaps a prepon-

derance of light, sporty bodies, the opposite proved to be the case. Out of the 502 cars in the first five batches laid down in 1933-34, only 30 were bodied as open tourers or similar.

All the remainder were either closed cars or drophead coupés, neither of which could be described as lightweight. As time went on these designs inevitably increased in weight rather than the reverse, with more luxurious seating, more padding and sound insulation, and the addition of such things as bumper bars, built-in jacks and radios. James Young, to take another example,

were understandably proud of their "parallel action" space-saving door, but its massive hinge mechanism must have added considerably to the weight of the body.

The design and experimental departments were concerned at this trend, and did what they could to encourage coachbuilders to keep weight down, preferably well below the company's limit of 8½cwt (430kg). However only Park Ward – and perhaps Vanden Plas with the tourer – could be said to be under the company's control, and other coach-builders were much more inclined to give in to customers' wishes than to resist. As it happened, the company had for some time been pursuing a development programme to increase the power of the Bentley engine. It now looked as if the time when such an engine would be needed was fast approaching.

3½ Litre – Summary Statistics

Engine

configuration	6 cylinders in line, overhead valves, pushrods
capacity	3669 cc
bore	3¼in (82.5mm)
stroke	4½in (114.3mm)
RAC rating	25.3hp
compression ratio	6.5:1
firing order	1 4 2 6 3 5
valve timing	io 3°btdc, ic 52° abdc, eo 49° bbdc, ec 6°atdc
tappet clearances	(cold) inlet .004in, exhaust .006in
brake horsepower	114 @ 4500rpm
crankshaft	
no of bearings	7
main bearing	2¼in(57mm) diameter
big end	2in (51mm) diameter
crankcase capacity	1½ galls (6.8 litres) – fill to 1¼ galls (5.7 litres)
cooling system	Water pump, thermostatic radiator shutters, capacity 3 galls (13.6 litres)
ignition details	Coil, 12 volts, with centrifugal and manual timing control
ignition timing	At "BAI" mark on flywheel
contact breaker gap	.015-.018in
plugs – make/gap	14mm, KLG FLB 30X / .015-.020in
carburettors	Twin 1⅜in SU
fuel pump	SU double-capacity electric
dynamo and charging system	Rolls-Royce, constant voltage control
starter motor	Rolls-Royce
clutch	Rolls-Royce, single plate, 10½ dia.
engine number location	On water pump bracket

Chassis

wheelbase	10ft 6in
track	4ft 8in
length	14ft 6in
width	5ft 9in
weight	2510lb (1140kg)
turning circle	42ft right, 40ft 8in left
wheels and tyres	Wire, splined hubs, India Speed Special 5.50 x 18 tyres
tyre pressures	35psi front/ 30psi rear
brake drums	12in diameter
steering box	Rolls-Royce, worm and nut
propellor shaft	Rolls-Royce, balanced, vibration damper

rear axle	Fully floating, hypoid bevel
ratio	4.1:1 or 3.91:1
oil capacity	1½ pints (0.85 litres)
shock absorbers	Rolls-Royce hydraulic (with speed control and driver override facility from chassis B1CW)
petrol tank capacity	18 galls/73 litres (16 galls main + 2 reserve)
chassis number location	On brass plate on bulkhead

Gearbox

type	Four speed, synchromesh on third and top
gear ratios	4.10, 5.10, 7.09 and 11.3 to 1, reverse 11.1:1. Alternative: 3.91, 4.87, 6.76 and 10.77 to 1, reverse 10.6:1
oil capacity	4½ pints (2.05 litres)

Prices

Chassis	£1100
Vanden Plas tourer	£1380
Park Ward 4-door saloon	£1460

Performance

Vanden Plas tourer	Max speed 91mph 0-60mph 18 seconds
Park Ward saloon	Max speed 91.8mph 0-60mph 20.4 seconds

Numbers Produced

1177

Top 10 coachbuilders

	Number of bodies
Park Ward	529 (428 saloons, 98 dhc, 3 other)
Thrupp & Maberly	111
Vanden Plas	77
H J Mulliner	64
Hooper	61
Barker	44
Freestone & Webb	39
Gurney Nutting	39
James Young	35
Arthur Mulliner	27
Others	144
Unknown	7
Total	**1177**

Chapter Five

The 4¼ Litre

The Park Ward saloon had by now gained the fashionable "falling waistline" but not yet an external petrol filler cap (chassis B228GA, June 1936).

The announcement, when it came, was so small it could easily have been missed. A single paragraph in *The Autocar* of 7 February 1936 merely said: "An alternative, larger-capacity engine in the Bentley chassis – that is the latest development announced by Bentley Motors (1931) Ltd. For £50 extra a 4¼-litre engine may be obtained in place of the 3½-litre. The chassis otherwise are identical. This move follows upon a number of requests for such a car. It will arouse huge interest." *The Motor* followed up the next week with a similar story, and added that the cylinder dimensions of the new engine were 88.5 x 114mm, giving a capacity of 4255cc and an RAC rating of 29.4hp.

We now know, of course, that the 4¼ Litre engine was a replacement for the 3½ Litre, and that the announcement was merely a subterfuge to console those customers who had already ordered the smaller-engined model and whose chassis were still at the coachbuilders. Hives and his team had been working on providing more power for the Bentley by some means or other, and the new engine was the outcome. It was always intended to supersede the 3½ Litre, and although the smaller engine remained nominally available to special order there is no record of this ever having

*The interior of the Park Ward standard saloon lost
nothing in luxury as time went on. This 4¼ Litre
dates from May 1937.*

Gurney Nutting's "pillarless coupé" of the late 1930s was light, airy and confident. This example was built around July 1937 on chassis B90KT.. See also pages 63, 76 and 82.

happened. Indeed the reverse was true, with the factory upgrading chassis already being completed and renumbering them as 4¼ Litre models.

Although enlarging the bore of the engine appears an obvious means of finding more power, the route to reaching that decision had in fact been a tortuous one. Hives and his team had initially wanted to explore supercharging once more, since this would avoid using larger and therefore heavier pistons which would increase the reciprocating

masses. In taking this view he was influenced by the increasing evidence of bearing problems, particularly at high engine speeds. Partly these could be attributed to crankshaft vibration which caused the flywheel to run out and damage the rear main bearing. A modified flywheel introduced during the life of the 3½-litre engine was aimed at curing this particular problem. Over and above this, however, it was clear that existing bearing materials were nearing the limit of their capacity,

however, were wary of supercharging in principle after their experience with the Bensport and Peregrine projects. Thus the decision came down in favour of increased engine capacity, and to do so by the simple means of increasing the bore size. This went up from 3¼in to 3½in (82.6 to 88.9mm), giving a cubic capacity of 4257cc. The RAC rated horsepower, which was dependent on bore size, also went up, from 25.3 to 29.4hp. However the tax rate had been reduced in the previous year by 25% (from £1 to 15 shillings per "horsepower"), so there

was less concern at this implication than there might have been. A prototype of the new engine was fitted in the hard-working chassis 1-B-IV, the first of the experimental cars, in early 1935 and started on a test programme.

Other engine improvements, including lessons learned from the Hall TT car, were incorporated at the same time. Bearing materials had to be revised, as it was known that white metal would not stand up to the increased loadings. Hall's car had used lead bronze, but amongst other things this required

B56JD, a four-door convertible or "all-weather", is variously ascribed to Offord, who were the coachwork suppliers, and Carlton, to whom Offord were sub-contracting most of their work by then (May 1937).

James Young first produced their "parallel action" swinging door in 1936. The example shown here is a 1937 car, chassis B74JD.

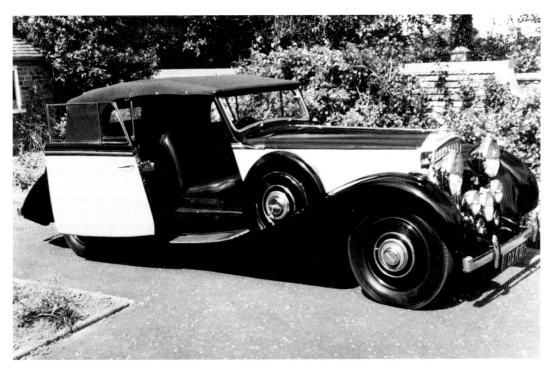

Further views of B90KT show details of its coachwork. Most, but not all, 4¼-litre models were fitted with an external petrol filler cap, as here. The boot and spare wheel treatment are typical of this coachbuilder, whereas the running-board strakes could almost have been "borrowed" from Vanden Plas!

large clearances which would not be suitable for production engines. The choice therefore fell on a material known as "Halls metal", named after not Eddie Hall but his namesake who was chief metal-lurgist at Derby. This was an aluminium/tin alloy, and it was used in the 4¼-litre engine for all the main and big end bearings. A further refinement, aimed at eliminating failures on numbers 2 and 5 big ends, was to improve their lubrication by cutting partial grooves in the intermediate main bearings. The compression ratio went up from 6.5 to 6.8:1, and breathing was improved by fitting larger carburettors and larger valves; inlet valve diameters went up from 1.5in to 1.7in, and exhaust from 1.425in to 1.525in. The size of the air silencer was also increased.

Apart from the engine, the remaining changes

One of the most elegant of all Mayfair's designs, this saloon is on chassis B107JY of May 1937.

were comparatively minor. To reduce the risk of fuel vapour lock the petrol filter on the bulkhead was replaced by twin filters located on the rear chassis cross-member. The Rolls-Royce designed clutch was changed to a bought-out Borg & Beck unit, an air-cooled dynamo was specified (and its drive gearing altered), and the exhaust cut-out was deleted. Standard and alternative rear axle ratios remained the same. The quoted power output of the new engine was now 125bhp, a worthwhile

increase over the 3½ Litre. There was a price increase of £50, making the bare chassis £1150 and the standard saloon £1510.

Deliveries of the new car started in the spring of 1936, and the motoring journals were eager to get their hands on demonstrators. First into print were *The Motor*, who tested a Park Ward saloon with the "optional" new engine. This was B3GA, the second 4¼ Litre chassis built, and converted from what would have been 3½ Litre chassis B83FC. "A defi-

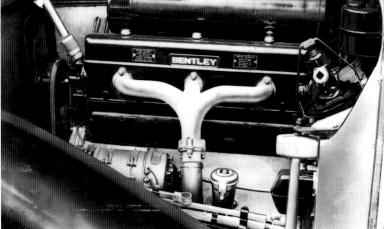

Left: *Exhaust side of the 4¼ Litre engine. Twin retaining straps for the dynamo are a quick recognition point compared with the 3½ Litre.*

Facing page
Top: *A more adventurous design than usual from Vanden Plas, this "saloon coupé" with dummy hood-irons on chassis B128KT was supplied to Austria in August 1937.*
Middle: *Thrupp & Maberly were starting to specialise in formal saloons. They built this design on chassis B199JY in June 1937.*
Bottom: *Windovers' 1937 Earls Court Show car was this rather rakish drophead coupé on chassis B121KU.*

B90KT's frontal view shows how by the later 1930s the front wings were taken down to the wheel centre-line, in an attempt to reduce air-resistance.

nite gain – and nothing lost" was their opening statement, and the remainder of the article bore it out. They had the advantage of having tested the smaller-engined car only five months previously, so its details were fresh in their minds. For the testers, the main improvements were that the acceleration was brisker, maximum speed was higher, and cruising at 70-75mph required a

smaller throttle opening than before. In terms of actual figures, the car reached a measured maximum speed of 96mph against 90mph previously, and accelerated from 0 to 50mph in 10.4 seconds compared with 12.8. These results are even more impressive when one realises that the 4¼ Litre saloon was heavier than the 3½ Litre drop-head coupé at 33½cwt (1700kg) versus 32½

A single centrally-mounted driving lamp was a standard fitting. The rearward-sloping "winged B" mascot is the correct one for the 4¼ Litre model, but the owner has to be careful to turn it through ninety degrees before he tries to open the bonnet!

Freestone & Webb, as the razor-edge pioneers, built numerous bodies in what they called their "brougham" style. This is their 1937 Earls Court Show car, chassis B131KU.

(1650kg). We might also note in passing that the nominally identical car – the standard Park Ward four-door, four-light saloon – which *The Autocar* tested two years earlier weighed only 30cwt (1525kg), so its weight had gone up by over 10%.

The speed-related hydraulic damping system came in for particular praise. "A point of special interest is the way in which the car followed the very abrupt contour which marks the top of Brooklands Test Hill. Here the gradient of 1 in 4 merges, in a couple of feet, into level ground. Even at a speed of over 30mph there was very little lifting at the back of the car, showing clearly the rapidity and power with which the special system of shock absorbers comes into action to check excessive spring movements." By contrast, there was some distinctly faint praise elsewhere. "The Bentley suspension and steering gear proved to be adequate in coping with the higher speeds attainable in the 4¼ Litre model". In the restrained parlance of a 1930s motoring journalist, this was surely code for "the suspension and steering are beginning to show their age". Nevertheless it was clear from the test as a whole that the car gave an outstanding overall impression.

Two weeks later *The Autocar* came out with their road test, which had been carried out on the same car as *The Motor's*. There was reasonably

close agreement on the acceleration figures, with *The Autocar* achieving 0-50mph and 0-60mph times of 10.3 and 15.5 seconds as against 10.4 and 14.8 from *The Motor*. What was surprising was their maximum speed of 90.9mph, where *The Motor* had obtained 96mph. However this was an average of runs in two directions, and their best one-way speed was 94.7mph. It would seem that at this period *The Motor* had only been taking one-way measurements, which could of course be affected by the wind. Otherwise there was not a breath of criticism, the writer observing that it was not sheer performance which counted, but the manner of it. "It is a wonderful experience to handle this car over main roads which give opportunity for employing the performance. The throttle goes down, and the speedometer needle sweeps round the dial; the landscape rushes past, but nothing else emphasises the rate of travel, and conversation in a normal voice can be continued."

Not to be outdone, *Motor Sport* carried out yet another test – the third on this same long-suffering car – for their June issue. Comparing the new model with its predecessor, they found a "quite unexpected increase of power" so that even the saloon-bodied car "sets up new standards of acceleration". In a very full and technically detailed write-up there was hardly a whiff of criticism, other than that the back of the driver's seat was too vertical. There was nevertheless a passing reference to "a certain amount of movement of the front wings" during high speed testing at Brooklands. Every other aspect of the car had praise heaped upon it, and the magazine's sporting readers were reminded of Mr E R Hall's achievements in the previous two TT races, and that the car was entered for that year's Le Mans. As to performance figures, these were always more sparse in *Motor Sport* tests, but acceleration from 0 to 60mph was accomplished in 13.5 seconds – a particularly good result – and the maximum one-way speed was 93mph. The writer's summary of the car was that it was "a magic carpet brought up to date".

As it happens the Le Mans race was cancelled that year (1936) because of labour troubles in France, but Eddie Hall entered the Tourist Trophy

for the third year running. He used B35AE once more, but it was modified still further, starting with the installation of a special 4¼-litre engine which had a 9:1 compression ratio and produced 167bhp. The petrol tank capacity, already raised to 32 gallons for the Le Mans race, was increased still further to 48 gallons. A new body – in fact a third body, since there had already been a new one fitted for Le Mans – was also deemed necessary, mainly to take advantage of a change in regulations which now permitted two-seater designs. The old (1934) body was mounted on chassis B106GA which became Hall's practice car. Rather embarrassingly, when after the race the Experimental department tested the two cars against each other at Brooklands, they showed that the older body was in fact the faster of the two. This did not stop Hall putting in another fine performance, finishing second on handicap yet again and setting the all-

Carlton built this Art Deco style pillarless saloon, on chassis B203 KU, to a design commissioned from Gurney Nutting. For the later history of this body, see pages 96 & 97.

This interior shot of B90KT gives the flavour of a gentleman's sporting carriage of the late 1930s. By this period the fashion for complicated fluting patterns in the leather trim was over, and instead there was often just a single pleat as here. Note also the fittings for the opening windscreen; British drivers' insistence on this feature ensured that their cars retained flat windscreens rather than following the Continental fashion for the vee variety.

The 4¼-litre engine is easily recognised by its longer air-cleaner. Access to the rear seat is good, although head- and leg-room are somewhat restricted.

Park Ward were another coach- builder to use razor- edge styling for some non-standard designs. This saloon is on chassis B166LS (September 1938).

time average speed record for the Ards circuit at 80.81mph.

During the summer *The Autocar* published an article comparing two 4¼ Litre cars which had been supplied to directors of their parent company – chassis B38GA and B100GA. Both were Park Ward four-door saloons, and both were so near to the standard design that the recital of detail differences was probably more interesting to the two owners than it was to the magazine's readers. However one significant point lay half-buried in the text. "Constructionally these Park Ward bodies represent something distinctly new in specialised body production, for steel enters largely into their manu- facture, and amongst other things is responsible for the narrow section of the screen pillars, which greatly assists visibility. Steel is also used for the panels and wings." No more could be said at that time, as Park Ward were not yet ready to give more details, but three months later they decided to reveal all.

The announcement in September of Park Ward's new system of all-steel construction was the culmi- nation of a problem which had been concerning both coachbuilders and specialist chassis manufac- turers for years. Coachbuilt bodies were increasingly being seen to perform badly in comparison with their mass-produced counterparts where durability, and therefore silence, were concerned. Not that the bodies on cheaper cars were totally rigid by any means, but their all-welded construction meant that they were becoming much less prone to develop faults. By contrast, when the

owner of a quality car with a coachbuilt body could report that no squeak or rattle had developed after a 2000-mile trip, it was regarded as an unusually fine achievement. *Automobile Engineer* in 1935 had put the point succinctly: "It is hardly reasonable to suppose that purchasers of high-priced vehicles will remain indifferent to faulty or noisy bodywork when perfect satisfaction is given by cars costing from a third to a half the price." They therefore concluded that "the builder even of hand-made bodies may be obliged to provide a virtually all- metal construction".

Rolls-Royce were in a unique position to try to solve the problem because of their close relation- ship, financial and otherwise, with Park Ward. From late 1934 onward the two companies worked together on a project to replace the traditional ash framework of a coachbuilt body with one made entirely from steel. They were by no means the first to attempt this, but no-one in recent years had got beyond using steel for a few key components of the framework. A prototype body, outwardly identical to the standard four-door saloon, was built on a 3½ Litre chassis, B56BN, and subjected to intensive testing on the Continent throughout 1935. Numerous further test bodies were built, one of which was the "coupé de ville" B135EJ which appeared on Park Ward's stand at the 1935 Olympia Show. There was no publicity about it at the time, and few were aware of its unusual construction. Two other early all-steel cars were of course the two belonging to the Iliffe directors, discussed above.

The system used a frame built up from fabricated steel ribs, which were pre-formed and then assembled using a combination of brazing and welding, to minimise distortion. Depending on the number of bodies to be made, the ribs and pillars could be shaped round cast iron formers, and wooden jigs used for final assembly. Mounting to the chassis was via Silentbloc bushes, and the panelling – necessarily steel rather than aluminium – was then attached by clinching over and spot-welding. The crucial element was the ability to form curves in the box-section ribs. These ribs were made by closing the flanges of a top-hat rolled steel section round a flat strip, in such a way that the strip was captive but could still slide within the flanges; the top-hat section was slotted at intervals along its length to facilitate bending. Thus the complete assembly could be formed into a curve, after which the two parts were brazed together. Park Ward's secrecy about these details may have been normal commercial caution, but may also have been because they did not want to reveal that the process had been invented not by themselves but by the three Meltz brothers, who thereafter acted as consultants to the firm.

Naturally in trying to solve the problem of body rigidity neither Rolls-Royce nor Park Ward wanted to aggravate the related problem of weight. The first prototype car did in fact weigh approximately the same at 32¾cwt (1665kg) as its ash-framed equivalent – understandably, as it was panelled in steel instead of aluminium. However by the end of 1935 a significant weight advantage had opened

up for the steel-framed body. Hives pointed out that for accurate comparisons the specifications had to be the same – for example, aluminium wings in each case – and on that basis the respective weights were 32¼cwt (1640kg) for the "steel" prototype and 33cwt (1675kg) for the standard ash-framed car. Some of that advantage must have been eroded by later modifications, since by the time the system was announced in September 1936 Park Ward were claiming a smaller (but still worthwhile) saving of half a hundredweight (25kg). They also maintained that the costs of the new method were no greater than before. Both *The Autocar* and *Automobile Engineer* were enthusiastic about the development, the latter periodical being of the opinion that it would have a major influence on the bodybuilding industry in the future. In the event they were probably more wrong than right, but at the time no-one would have disagreed with them.

At the Motor Show which followed Park Ward made no secret of their all-steel Bentley bodies, which attracted much attention. There were once again 17 different Bentleys scattered around the show, even though the number of exhibitors was gradually declining. Bentley's own stand contained their usual three standard offerings – two from Park Ward and one from Vanden Plas. Interestingly, the fixed-head coupé on the Barker stand also boasted steel framing, but in their case it was still combined with ash. It was beginning to look as if it was only the Bentley marque which was keeping the coachbuilding industry in existence. At

A superb late '30s design, this concealed-head coupé with dickey was built by James Young in July 1938.

We saw this body previously, on page 91, fitted to its original chassis B203KU. For some reason it was later transferred to chassis B55GP (previously a Rippon saloon), which is the form in which we see it here – after a full restoration which included a two-tone paint job. Carlton used an identical body, on chassis B77KU, as their exhibit at the 1937 Earls Court Show.

The lack of running-boards and "full-width" rear are typical of the period – as is the Lalique mascot.

the next Show in 1937, the first to be held at Earls Court, the number of Bentley exhibits had gone up to 20, including new users Carlton and Windovers. Even in 1938, with major firms such as Barker being taken over and Arthur Mulliner withdrawing from the business, there were 17 Bentleys there as against only 12 Rolls-Royces. (Full details of all the exhibits including chassis numbers are listed in Appendix 1.)

In May of 1937 Geoffrey Smith – editor of *The Autocar*, and one of the Iliffe directors referred to above – published his opinions on the differences between the 3½ and 4¼ Litre cars. Smith was in a good position to know, having consumed Bentleys at the rate of one per year since the launch. His assessment of the power increase was that the new model had the same rate of acceleration in top gear as the old one had in third. Maximum speed was unchanged, as it should be, since the gearing was the same and so was the engine speed limit (4500rpm). However it was the acceleration which

was the more important, since it determined how quickly you regained your cruising speed. Fuel consumption was 1mpg worse, and tyre life was slightly reduced (16,000 miles compared with 18,000). The car's silence and lightness of controls made 400-mile journeys no hardship: "London to Glasgow is a comfortable day's jaunt between breakfast and dinner".

During 1937 both *The Motor* and *The Autocar* ran another test of the 4¼ Litre, each using the same car (DXM222, chassis B119JY). Why they should have found a second test necessary is unclear, unless it was to inspect the all-steel construction of the saloon. *The Motor* noted that it had grown in both internal width and roof height – but not, apparently, in weight, thus bearing out Park Ward's claims. An acceleration time of 10.8 seconds from 0 to 50mph was in line with all previous tests, as was their measured (but one-way) maximum speed of 91mph. The testers permitted themselves a few gentle criticisms, for example about the tendency of the servo brakes

H J Mulliner were another firm who built some concealed-head versions of drophead coupés. This example also dates from 1938.

26357

to lock the rear wheels at low speeds. There was also a comment about the ease or otherwise of exit through the driver's door while negotiating the right-hand brake and gear-change levers, an arrangement which was starting to look idiosyncratic.

The Autocar tested the car some time later, but did not even comment on the new coachwork. Interestingly, they made mild criticisms in the same two areas – the right-hand levers getting in the way of exit, and the brakes. In the latter case their comment was that there was a slight delay in the braking action when one was reversing (this was a quirk which was inherent in the design of the servo mechanism) Their acceleration figures were well down, to the extent that one wonders whether the car had had a hard life in the intervening five months: their 0 to 50 and 0 to 60mph figures were 12.7 and 17.1 seconds respectively. Measured maximum speed was 88mph, but their best one-way run achieved 91.8mph, thus both endorsing *The Motor*'s findings and underlining that *The Autocar*'s test method was more accurate.

During the nearly two years that the 4¼ Litre had been in production there had been a number of changes to its specification. As far as the driver was concerned, he would have found a new switch on the instrument panel whereby he could use one or other petrol pump, or (in normal running) both together, a facility which allowed him to test the pumps individually. Another addition was a fuel warning light, which replaced the previous reserve

tap. There were other changes under the bonnet, however, that he would not have known about. Some work in the Experimental department had found that the "turbulated" head design, which used the lips of the "bathtub" combustion chamber to provoke turbulence and optimise mixing, was causing detonation (knocking). A revised design both eliminated the problem and resulted in a small power increase, even though the compression ratio was reduced slightly (to 6.4:1). The bottom end of the engine also received some attention, with yet more changes in bearing specifications, including a reversion to white metal for the rear main. Lubrication changes, aimed at curing big end failures at high engine speeds, included drilling a second hole in each crankpin and increasing the capacity of the pump.

Without doubt the problem which concerned the company most at this period was crankshaft vibration. The Bentley engine, and therefore its crankshaft, were long by modern standards, having been adapted from the Rolls-Royce 20/25hp. While this latter car, with its peak engine speed of 3/50rpm, experienced no problems, the Bentley engine with its better breathing could be taken to much higher speeds – uncomfortably close to where the "master" crankshaft vibration period occurred. It was for this reason that the revolution counter was red-lined at 4500rpm, but even this speed only just avoided the onset of the vibration period, and the company was obliged to warn its

One of the early "overdrive" chassis (B76MR), this Vanden Plas continental tourer is illustrated in its modern guise on pages 113 and 116-7.

A 1936 Hooper design of "coupé cabriolet" (three-position dropbead coupé, in other words) on chassis B18HK.

Facing page: Hooper's craftmansbip was always of the higbest quality, while their designs were classic rather than innovative.

owners about the dangers of continuous high-speed driving (such as on the newly-built autobahns and autostradas). Something more was clearly required, which would take at least the top gear engine speed well below the danger zone. The result was the so-called "overdrive" model, announced in October 1938 in time for the Motor Show.

The heart of these cars, known sometimes as the "M" series from their chassis numbers, is a completely new gearbox. Top now becomes an indirect ratio which gears up the input speed at a ratio of 0.85:1, while third gear is the direct drive. The remaining ratios are 1.49:1 and 2.38:1. At the same time the rear axle ratio is lowered slightly, from 4.1 to 4.3:1. The net effect of these changes is to give a much higher ratio in the "overdrive" top gear at 3.64:1, equivalent to 26mph per 1000rpm. At the same time third gear is closely equivalent to the old top, so that it can be used as such while

reserving the true top gear for periods of steady running at high speed. This effectively ensures that the engine cannot be mistreated when the car is in top gear, but it leaves open the possibility that the 4500rpm limit could be exceeded in the lower gears. As a further precaution against such treatment, therefore, the cam profiles have been modified to ensure that power delivery drops off sharply above 4200rpm, so that there is nothing to be gained by hanging on to an intermediate gear above this speed.

Other changes were introduced at the same time, the most important of these being a Marles cam and roller steering box in place of the worm and nut box of Rolls-Royce manufacture, the new box having a slightly lower ratio. Experience had shown that the previous set-up, though perfectly acceptable when new, was both sensitive to castor angle changes and prone to "stickiness" when the

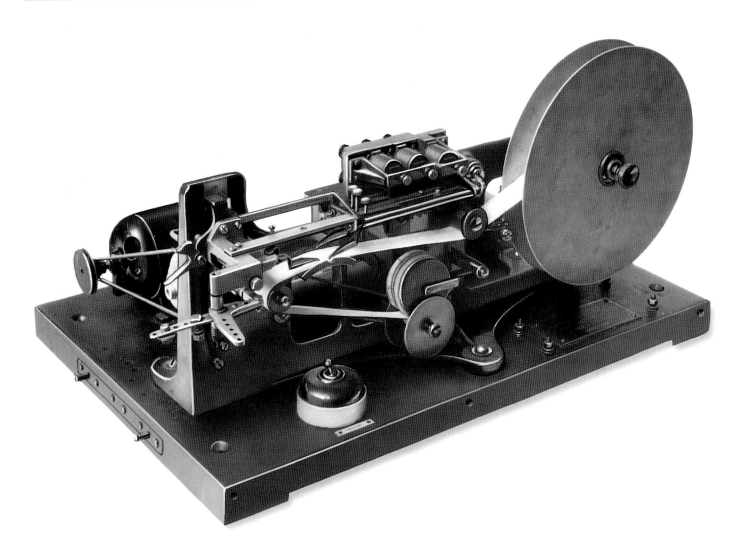

nut became slightly worn. Thermostatic radiator shutters were done away with, and the cooling system was controlled instead by a thermostat within the circulation system. The rear axle assembly was strengthened, including larger-diameter half shafts. Wheels were reduced in diameter from 18 to 17 inches, and the rolling radius was restored by specifying 6.50 section tyres in place of 5.50. On the instrument panel the oil pressure and water temperature gauges were combined into one, the clock became electric instead of wind-up, the fuel warning light was changed from red to green and an electrical master switch was added. The panel itself was completely rearranged, with the speedometer in the middle, surrounded by the smaller instruments, and the switch-panel moved to the right of the steering column alongside the rev counter. The instruments themselves were given concave dials and improved illumination at night.

The Autocar gave some immediate impressions of driving the car, without carrying out a full road test. They correctly summed up the reasons for the new model being developed. "Clearly, one of the advantages of the new transmission, quite apart from the added sense of ease at ordinarily fast speeds, is that the car can be driven on full throttle for indefinite periods on the Continental roads in the knowledge that the engine is not being over-stressed." They also complimented the new steering layout, saying that it was "appreciably lighter than before", and the bigger tyres, which they thought (not surprisingly) improved the ride.

This was the period when Rolls-Royce were showing increasing concern about their image with the buying public. An impression was abroad that they were far more interested in aero engine production than in developing their cars, and the company felt they needed to do something about

Another piece of testing apparatus in use at Rolls-Royce was this early type of recording accelerometer.

Another Hooper "coupé cabriolet", on chassis B94JD, uses a quite different approach from B18HK. This is a concealed-head version, with a totally different – and arguably prettier – rear- end treatment. Positioning the spare wheel in the wing rather than on the boot lid gives much more scope for a streamlined tail; the penalty is reduced boot space – hence the luggage rack.

The Hooper designer (presumably the famous Osmond Rivers) has achieved that rare feat - a drophead which is as attractive with the hood up as down. (For comparison, look at the designs illustrated on pages 95 and 98.) The integration of the waistline into the rear wing, and the matching slope of the hood, are particularly well handled.

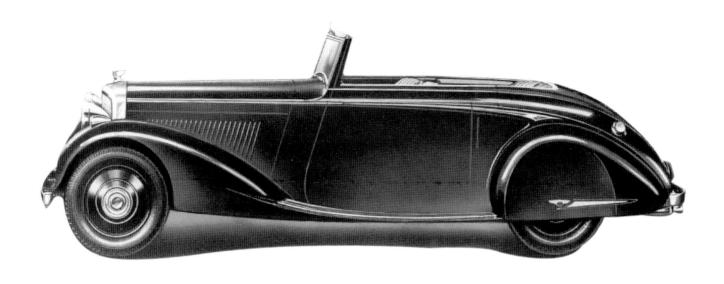

Top: *Park Ward built this concealed-head drophead coupé on "overdrive" chassis B16MR for the Bentley stand at the 1938 Earls Court Show.* Above: *For comparison, this is the standard Park Ward drophead coupé as it appeared on the M-series chassis.*

it. An immediate reaction was actively to seek publicity for the unseen things that went on at Derby, especially the degree of testing which every part went through, and which was unlikely to be matched by any other British manufacturer. Sure enough, early in 1939 there appeared in *The Autocar* two articles entitled "The Third Degree", which went into great detail about the destructive and other testing which went on in the Experimental department. Then *The Motor* followed up with "Developments in High-Duty Bearings", which sang the praises of the company's expertise in metallurgy. The technical detail in these articles was impressive, and must have helped to achieve the company's objective in enhancing their reputation for quality.

Behind this objective, though, was a very real concern about the strength of the competition. Neither Lagonda nor Alvis had been standing still, and there was a newcomer – SS Jaguar – who offered frighteningly good value for money. Lagonda design was now of course in the hands of WO Bentley, and from limited resources he was coming up with some excellent motor cars. In his hands the M45 had become firstly the much more refined LG45, with synchromesh on the upper three gears, and then the LG6 with independent front suspension and hydraulic brakes. More than that, Lagonda had also introduced their V12 model, to which Bentley had no response. Alvis had uprated their performance with the introduction of their 3½ Litre and Speed 25 models, and then

matched Bentley's increase in engine size with their "4.3", all these models boasting both synchromesh on all four gears and independent front suspension. Technically, therefore, the Bentley was beginning to be left behind.

In sheer performance, too, Bentley's lead had been eroded. The company's sensitivity in this area was demonstrated when the two leading motoring magazines, *The Autocar* and *The Motor*, tested 4¼ Litre cars in the spring of 1939. *The Autocar*, testing a standard Park Ward saloon, were more than usually sycophantic in their praise, while *The Motor*, with a drophead coupé by Vanden Plas, were complimentary in most respects, but thought that the ride was "on the hard side on secondary roads", and also mumbled some reservations about the brakes. In terms of performance figures, the results were broadly similar between the two magazines, those from the drophead being marginally inferior. However Rolls-Royce clearly persuaded themselves that *The Motor*'s car was below par, and prevailed upon the magazine to repeat the test. The new figures were duly published three weeks later, and although they showed some improvement the differences were marginal, and the car's maximum speed was still inferior to that of the saloon.

Even using the saloon's figures the Bentley had a job to hold its head up against its competition, with a maximum speed of 89mph as compared with 91mph and 100mph for the LG6 and V12 Lagonda saloons respectively and 96mph for the

Alvis 4.3 saloon. The Bentley's 0-60mph acceleration time was 15.6 seconds, whereas the two Lagondas recorded 16.0 and 12.9 seconds respectively and the Alvis achieved 13.1 seconds. And these performances were from cars which, apart from the V12 Lagonda, cost less than the £1535 Bentley, with the two Lagondas priced at £1550 (V12) and £1195 (LG6) and the Alvis at £995. Furthermore, below these rarified price levels there were of course a number of other marques anxious to attract the buyer of sporting machinery. None gave more concern to Rolls-Royce than the company which only a few years previously had been the Swallow Coachbuilding Co, was now called SS Cars Ltd and made a car called the Jaguar. In 1939 their largest-engined saloon model, the 3½ litre, was tested at 88mph and achieved a 0 to 60mph acceleration time of 14.4 seconds. Yet it cost a mere £445, and as a result was selling well – 1300 over the two-year period.

Some car snobs looked down on the Jaguar, but Rolls-Royce had the greatest respect for what the SS company had achieved. In late 1937 Robotham got himself invited to tour the Jaguar factory. (In all the correspondence the company is referred to as "Jaguar", and with the dropping of the SS1 and SS2 one suspects that the man in the street was beginning to refer to them by that name as well.) His visit included a drive in the then-new 3½ litre, and he immediately made a full report on what he had seen. Naturally crankshaft vibration was of intense interest, and Robotham estimated that the Jaguar's

Park Ward exhibited this fixed-head coupé on chassis B30MR, finished in maroon, on their own stand at the 1938 Show.

The Hooper coupé cabriolet (B94JD) has had every conceiveble extra added (probably by later owners) including wheel discs, spot lamp, windscreen visors and bumper overriders.

The radio is also a later addition, although many cars were fitted with them as new.

Chassis B8MR, one of the first "overdrive" 4¼ Litre models, went to France to be bodied by the firm of De Villars as a fixed-head coupé. It then went on their stand at the 1938 Paris Salon. Its lines are more formal than one normally associates with this type of body.

Hooper, still the most respected firm in coachbuilding, produced this sports saloon on chassis B134MR in March 1939. There is just a trace of razor-edge influence.

master vibration period did not occur until nearly 6000rpm. He attributed this mainly to the fact that the engine was two inches shorter than the Bentley's, because they had eliminated water passages between the bores, and also to the engine having a much lighter flywheel. "At all speeds the engine appeared to be appreciably smoother than the Bentley". Jaguar told him that their twin exhaust system helped power development particularly at intermediate speeds. Robotham commented on the good finish of the engine, and also on the fact that their chassis, like the Bentley's, was not cross-braced – although it should be noted that, unlike the Bentley's, it was heavily boxed-in.

The immediate outcome was that Rolls-Royce bought a 3½-litre saloon for evaluation. It did not arrive until March, and as soon as it was run in it was rushed down to Brooklands, where it lapped in a respectable 84.81mph. Then the car was dismantled and each part inspected and weighed, with key components drawn as well. After the car was reassembled an initial decision to sell it on was rescinded and instead it stayed in the company for long-term evaluation. Meanwhile Robotham used the information they had obtained to carry out a full cost analysis, and some of the results were discomfiting. As an example, they

discovered that Rolls-Royce were paying twice as much for their crankshaft forgings as Jaguar were, even though the R-R design was less complicated.

The other side of the Jaguar story is that the car proved less than reliable. In some six months of running up to October 1938, it suffered a leaking petrol tank, broken exhaust pipe, leaking battery, faulty silencer, stripped tooth in the gearbox and a broken brake rod – and this with a mileometer reading only 8100 miles. All the faulty components were replaced under guarantee. There was more to the story, however. The car had been taken to Brooklands again in September, where it recorded 87.22mph for the flying half-mile. The next month there is a curt note in the file about picking the car up, ending with "the pistons are on the back seat"; there had been a catastrophic engine failure involving a dropped valve. Robotham asked Jaguar to make amends (even though the car was by now out of guarantee), and managing director William Lyons refused, convinced that the car had been thrashed beyond normal use. In the end Robotham had to back down.

In terms of sales of Bentley cars, Rolls-Royce had nothing to be ashamed about. From its introduction in 1933 to the end of the model's life, the 3½ Litre had sold some 1180 examples, and the 4¼ Litre up to but not including the overdrive model

had added some 930 – a total in round numbers of 2100. This was far more than either of their main rivals had achieved in the same market segment: Lagonda sales of equivalent models over the same period were probably no more than 1000, and for Alvis the total was about 1300. Nevertheless the Bentley was beginning to look old-fashioned technically, and this coupled with its high price meant that sales could only go one way unless the car was updated soon. Company insiders certainly had no illusions, as Elliott had made clear back in March 1937 when he drove the steel saloon proto-type: "This car is excellent for demonstrating the lack of rigidity of the present Bentley chassis, and is generally very unpleasant and uncomfortable in any position of the ride control". His comments make clear that the senior management had few illusions about the chassis, which had originated from the much smaller Peregrine project and which, in that process, might even have shed an engine sub-frame.

Elliott was only reinforcing what many had been saying for a year or more. In March 1936 Robotham had circulated a paper titled "Independent Springing on the Bentley", which is worth quoting from in some detail. "Personally we feel that in 18 months' time it will be very difficult to sell a £1500 car without the comfort obtainable

with this [front] suspension. Already owners of our products have compared our suspension unfavourably with that of the even keel ride provided by Humbers. [Humber's ifs system was marketed as Evenkeel.] We should like to tackle the problem in two ways: (1) Improve the present Bentley frame as far as possible with the minimum modification. The object of improving the frame is to enable us to fit low rating road springs to give a comfortable ride without running into 'tramp' – our present limitation. A stiff frame would also enable us to employ a roll rod [ie anti-roll bar] to regain any road holding qualities which might be lost with the low rating front springs. . . . (2) Get all the information we can from the only sample available of torsion rod springing, as per the attached memo." This memo set out a proposal to obtain Citroen front suspension parts, and manufacture longer torsion bars, in order to produce a test chassis with independent front suspension. Behind this project was frustration at the delay in devel-oping an alternative design which used coil springs, and which eventually won the day. The reference to "improving the frame" involved a project to box in the frame's side channels to increase their stiffness, as a stopgap measure before the arrival of either ifs or at least cruciform bracing to stiffen the chassis even more.

Vanden Plas managed to combine the modern convex form of front wing with running boards in this four-seat tourer on chassis B172MR in May 1939.

It was common practice for Continental buyers to order right hand drive cars. The instrument panel on "overdrive" cars differs from previous 4¼ Litre cars, with the speedometer in the centre of the dashboard and the revolution counter to the right of the steering column.

The somewhat square lines of the De Villars coupé provide excellent headroom at the rear.

Below is another "overdrive" chassis, B76MR, which we have already seen on page 99. Here the Vanden Plas continental tourer is seen in its present-day colours.

B69MX

H J Mulliner built this well-proportioned design (listed as a fixed-head coupé, but looking remarkably like a pillarless saloon) on chassis B69MX in July 1939.

Other tests were suggesting new lines of development. Mr Gordon Armstrong, owner of the Armstrong Patent Suspension Co Ltd, allowed the Experimental department to try out his otherwise standard Bentley, which was fitted with independent front suspension and shock-absorbers of his own manufacture. "We took the car over the Ashbourne-Buxton road, a stretch which closely approaches Continental conditions in that it normally accentuates all the worst suspension features of the Bentley. We were astonished at the results achieved. From the point of view of the front and rear occupants' comfort, and the directional control of the driver, the car was in an entirely different class to any Bentley we have previously tried fitted with a similar type of body." From this one test would emerge an entirely new front suspension layout.

At the same time tests on the newly-built skid pan were bringing new insights into a car's behaviour. It was only now that the words understeer and oversteer began to enter the testers' vocabulary, and the effect which differential tyre pressures could have on this phenomenon was beginning to be understood. "The Skid Pan enables us when choosing a new section of tyre to make sure in a few minutes that we do not standardise a tyre sensitive to tyre pressures from the point of view of handling, a fault very evident on the Packard". The

3½ Litre car was judged to understeer, whereas the 4¼ Litre, with its added weight more on the back axle, had become an oversteerer. "The Bentley car fitted with Gordon Armstrong independent front suspension understeered. On the road it handled very well, the steering being far more accurate than a standard Bentley".

As to improving the car's performance, the company was prepared to think radically. As early as 1934, under a designer named Tresilian, there was an investigation of an overhead camshaft design, using first a gear drive and then a conventional chain. Even after Tresilian moved to Lagonda in 1936 to work under W O Bentley the project continued, to the point of building at least one test engine. It had an aluminium head and a compression ratio of 6.5:1, and produced 158bhp, which was a substantial increase over the pushrod engine. On the debit side it suffered from detonation, there were problems with the head gasket and the camshaft drive was deemed noisy. Modified cam profiles helped alleviate the latter problem, but the project was eventually shelved in favour of the inlet-over-exhaust valve layout.

So the limitations of the 4¼ Litre car began to be ever more apparent, at least to the Design and Experimental staff, and a new model which would overcome them was becoming an ever more urgent requirement. It should have a more powerful engine, a stiffer chassis and independent front suspension, and ideally its gearbox should do better than have synchromesh on just two gears. At the same time its weight should be no more than that of the current car, and preferably less. Yet in spite of the best efforts of everyone involved, this paragon of a motor car would not be ready until well into 1939.

4¼ Litre – Summary Statistics

Engine

configuration	6 cylinders in line, overhead valves, pushrods
capacity	4257cc
bore	3½in (88.9mm)
stroke	4½in (114.3mm)
RAC rating	29.4hp
compression ratio	6.8:1 (6.4:1 from chassis B101KU)
firing order	1 4 2 6 3 5
valve timing	io 3° btdc, ic 52° abdc, eo 49° bbdc, ec 6° atdc
	overdrive model io @ tdc, ic 45½° abdc, eo 43½° bbdc, ec @ tdc
tappet clearances	(cold) inlet and exhaust .004in
	overdrive model inlet .004in, exhaust .006in
brake horsepower	125bhp @ 4500rpm (4200rpm from B2MR)
crankshaft	
no of bearings	7
main bearing	2¼in (57mm) diameter
big end	2in (51mm) diameter
oil capacity	1½ galls (6.8 litres) fill to 1¼ galls (5.7 litres)
cooling system	water pump, thermostatic radiator shutters (in-line thermostat on overdrive model)
capacity	3 galls (13.6 litres)
ignition details	Coil, 12 volts, with centrifugal and manual timing control
ignition timing	Set at "BAI" mark on flywheel
contact breaker gap	.015-.018in
plugs – make/gap	14mm, KLG FLB 30X / .015-.020in, overdrive model .018in
carburettors	Twin 1⅜in SU
fuel pump	SU double-capacity electric
dynamo and charging system	Rolls-Royce air-cooled, constant voltage control
starter motor	Rolls-Royce
clutch	Borg & Beck, 10in diameter
engine number location	On water pump bracket

Chassis

wheelbase	10ft 6in
track	4ft 8in
length	14ft 6in
width	5ft 9in
weight	2558lb (1160kg)
turning circle	42 ft right, 40 ft 8in left
wheels and tyre size	Wire, splined hubs, India Super 18 x 5.50 tyres, overdrive model India Silent 17 x 6.50 tyres
tyre pressures	35psi front/ 30psi rear, overdrive model 23psi front/26psi rear
brake drum diameter	12in

steering box	Rolls-Royce, worm and nut. Marles cam and roller from B2MR (overdrive model)
propellor shaft	Rolls-Royce, balanced, vibration damper
rear axle	Fully floating, hypoid bevel
ratio	4.1:1 or 3.91:1. 4.3:1 from B2MR (overdrive model)
oil capacity	1½ pints (0.85 Litres)
shock absorbers	Rolls-Royce hydraulic with speed control and driver override facility
petrol tank capacity	18 galls/73 litres (16 galls main + 2 reserve)
chassis number location	On brass plate on bulkhead

Gearbox

type	Four speed, synchromesh on third and top
gear ratios	4.10, 5.10, 7.09 and 11.3 to 1 – reverse 11.1:1 Alternative: 3.91, 4.87, 6.76 and 10.8 to 1 – reverse 10.6:1. Overdrive model 3.64, 4.3, 6.43 and 10.2 to 1
oil capacity	4½ pints (2.05 litres), overdrive model 4 pints (1.8 litres)

Prices

chassis	£1150
Vanden Plas tourer	£1430
Park Ward 4-door saloon	£1510

Performance

Park Ward saloon	Max speed 91.8mph, 0-60mph 17.1 seconds
Park Ward saloon (overdrive)	Max speed 92.8mph, 0-60mph 16.1 seconds

Numbers Produced

1234

Top 10 coachbuilders

	Number of bodies
Park Ward	530 (473 saloons, 51 dhc, 6 other)
Vanden Plas	122
Thrupp & Maberly	105
H J Mulliner	102
Gurney Nutting	50
Hooper	45
Van Vooren	44
Freestone & Webb	37
James Young	35
Barker	24
Others	131
Unknown	9
Total	**1234**

B76MR, the Vanden Plas continental tourer, was exhibited at the 1938 Brussels and Geneva shows. The philosophy behind such a design was that it should fulfil two roles – completely open for summer touring, yet as watertight as a saloon in inclement weather.

The overdrive 4¼ Litre engine has a plain oil-filler cap (no "B" badge), not to mention a thermostat in the cooling system. This car boasts a full set of tools, including the jack mounted on the scuttle. A spare coil was still part of the specification.

Chapter Six

The Mark V

The Mark V model was planned for launch at the 1939 London Motor Show. It differs significantly from the 4¼ Litre, and many of these changes were made, as we have seen, in order to overcome perceived shortcomings in the previous model. But there was another set of influences at work at the same time, namely the move towards a "rationalised range". This buzz-word encompassed a policy, begun during 1938, to maintain and enhance the company's competitiveness through a substantial lowering of production costs. This would be achieved by limiting the number of models in the Bentley/Rolls-Royce range, and then building them as far as possible from common components (90% interchangeability was the target) and common production processes. The Mark V Bentley was the first step down this road, and even then only a partial one, but it was a beginning. To take just one example, the new model was given a wheelbase of 10ft 4in, a reduction of two inches, which one might think was a retrograde step. However this was to align it with the three standard wheelbase dimensions of the rationalised range – 10ft 4in, 10in 10in and 11ft 1in. Engines, too, were to be "rationalised", using the inlet over exhaust layout, and the final new range was going to be launched at the 1940 Motor Show.

As things turned out there would be no Motor Show in either 1940 or 1939, and no rationalised range either then or later. Indeed, very few Mark Vs would be produced at all, and of these many were chassis which were never bodied and which were then scrapped; it is thought that only nine cars

survive. Nevertheless in many ways the model crystallised the direction in which the Bentley marque wanted to go, and can be regarded as the immediate forerunner of the postwar Mark VI. Its name derives from the "V" series of chassis numbers given to the experimental cars, which were numbered 7-B-V and so on as the next logical series after the 4¼ Litre prototype 6-B-IV. There were no less than seven Mark V prototypes, although it is thought that only three were used for extensive testing, the others being converted to test various components such as engines. Testing began in early 1938, and was completed a year later.

Perhaps the most fundamental change introduced with the Mark V is the design of the chassis frame itself. Up to this point the Bentley had been struggling with a light, flexible frame inherited from the Peregrine project, which had always been intended to be a light car of moderate performance. The limitations of that frame had only been overcome by scrupulous attention to damping, and even that was now insufficient. The Mark V frame is therefore very much stronger, firstly because its side channel-section members are deeper (7½in instead of 6½in) but secondly, and more importantly, because it is at last diagonally braced – and very substantially so. This cross-bracing runs virtually the whole length of the interior of the chassis, from the raised portion over the rear axle up to the pressed-steel bulkhead.

Thereafter there is additional bracing in the form of diagonal channel-section members, which stiffen the forward part of the chassis and virtually

12-B-V, one of the experimental Mark V chassis. This particular one was fitted with a special lightweight Park Ward saloon body.

The Jaguar saloon was used as a benchmark during development of the Mark V, as a means of ensuring that weight was kept to a minimum.

Mark V chassis B30AW was one of only nine (it is believed) to have been completed to specification – the remainder having been either modified and used as experimental chassis or broken up. The body is by H J Mulliner.

turn it into a box section.

At the front there is another innovation in the form of independent front suspension, which had been introduced on the Rolls-Royce Phantom III and the recently launched Wraith, but which was new to Bentley. Its design differs from those two models, and is evidently modelled on that of the contemporary Packard. This was supposedly the only American design Rolls-Royce could find that could be adapted to their particular requirements – specifically, where rubber bushing could be added to reduce noise without compromising the steering. This suspension could be regarded as double wishbone if one can count the forked arm of an Armstrong shock absorber as a wishbone.

This touches on yet another change from the 4¼ Litre, whereby the Rolls-Royce designed hydraulic shock absorbers with their speed- and driver-controlled pressure were deleted in favour of the Armstrong version at the front while being retained at the back. Coil springs are used as the springing medium, although as we saw in the last chapter an alternative layout using torsion bars was considered at one stage of development. The lower "wishbone" is made up of two separate arms joined at their outer ends, with the rear arm pivoted far back along the chassis so as to act as a brake torque reaction member. The two suspension units are connected by an anti-roll bar, and rubber bushing is used throughout. The rear suspension continues to use long semi-elliptic leaf springs, but a radius arm has been added on the off side which controls both torque reaction and the axle's arc of movement – the latter in order to prevent any reaction on the rod brakes, of which more later.

At the front of the chassis the designers fell into line with what was by then current practice, and moved the engine and radiator much further forward – in the case of the engine, by a matter of five inches. This more than compensated for the reduction in wheelbase, and the increased passenger space available allowed footwells to be eliminated. The radiator sits on top of the front suspension cross-member and has its own filler concealed under the bonnet, the external filler cap being a dummy. The engine, although of the same cylinder dimensions as before (3½in bore and 4½in stroke) is a new design. Essentially a modified Rolls-Royce Wraith unit, its cross-flow head has four inlet ports instead of six with the middle pairs siamesed; peak power output is 125bhp at 3800rpm. The crankshaft is substantially stronger

B30AW was intended to be exhibited at the 1939 London Show, which never took place. It was used as a Rolls-Royce company car throughout World War Two.

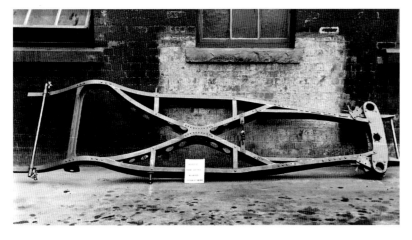

Top: *The long-suffering experimental chassis 4-B-IV, heavily modified (probably during 1936) by the substitution of Citroën torsion-bar front suspension.*
Above: *An early experimental Mark V chassis frame, differing from the final version only in small alterations to the front cross-member.*

than the 4¼ Litre's, with main journals of bigger diameter and thicker webs. In compensation, the width of both main and big end bearings is reduced, thus avoiding any increase in the engine's overall length. The main bearings revert to white metal, while the big ends use a variation of the "Halls metal" alloy known as AC9.

As an additional measure to counter crankshaft vibration, a revised design of flywheel is used . This is essentially a flexible steel disc with most of the mass concentrated at the rim. The principle is that the rim acts as a gyroscope and maintains its orbit, so that crankshaft oscillations merely cause the disc to flex and are thus damped out. Forged connecting rods are a new design in nickel steel, and the Aerolite pistons also differ from before in having horizontal slits below the bottom ring. An aluminium crankcase and cast iron block are the same in principle, but there are a number of detailed changes to the block. These include realigning the pushrods because of a change to the

arrangement of the valves in the head, which in turn have been repositioned so that they use a common design of rocker arm. Another change to the block is brought about by a total revision to the camshaft and auxiliary drives, following a relocation of the distributor and oil pump to the near side. These two are now in front of the dynamo and water pump, and so the drive arrangement only requires three gears instead of five. It was found that the addition of the water pump to this driveline acted as a form of damper, and so the separate dynamo damper has been eliminated. The oil pump is a new type of higher capacity, and it incorporates a second stage pressure relief valve which allows a constant lower-pressure feed to the valve gear. For the first time there is a bypass oil filter with a renewable element. The exhaust manifold is still a three branch design, but modified somewhat to pass behind the repositioned dynamo.

On the inlet side, the manifold is new but is still water-heated, and there are again twin SU carburettors. The rear carburettor now has an auxiliary starting device which is electrically operated and which cuts out automatically. Both the air cleaner and its trunking are changed. The twin coils – working plus spare – remain on the inlet (off) side of the engine. The engine as a whole rests on twin mounting points as before, but the front one is elevated by means of a large A-bracket, offset slightly from the engine centre line and attached to the engine via rubber. The rear mounting point takes the form of a bracket on the back of the gearbox, with extended arms each side which are attached, again via rubber, to the chassis diagonals. This arrangement, clearly based on the Chrysler "Floating Power" concept, places the engine's axis of movement through its centre of gravity and thus minimises the impact of any rocking motion.

The clutch is also new, having light springs backed up by centrifugally weighted withdrawal levers, and drives a gearbox that is also totally new. Top is still an overdrive gear, but synchromesh is now provided on second as well as the upper two gears. There is some confusion about the ratios; the drawing shows 0.836:1, 1:1, 1.43:1, and 2.44:1, and these figures are confirmed by a description in Automobile Engineer in 1941, whereas an Autocar article some months earlier gives 0.847:1, 1:1, 1.50:1 and 2.38:1. The rear axle ratio is 4.3:1, as for the overdrive 4¼ Litre. The ride control oil pump serving the rear shock absorbers is now incorporated inside the gearbox, and the brake servo

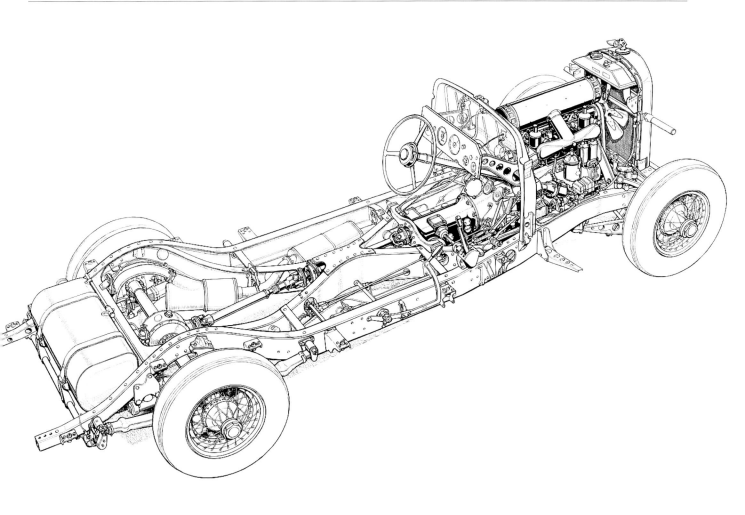

motor moves to the right-hand (off) side.

Output from the gearbox is now via a divided propellor shaft, the centre bearing for which is located just behind the centre of the diagonal cross bracing. The rear axle assembly on the early cars is still a fully floating unit with wire wheels, but the intention under the "rationalised range" policy was to move to a semi-floating design with pressed steel wheels to save both weight and cost. Wheel diameter is 16in, using 6.50 x 16 tyres. The braking system is totally different, using rods instead of cables and operating on a modified form of Girling mechanism. Great care has been taken in the layout of the system at front and back to ensure that it remains unaffected by either wheel movement or axle wind-up, including the radius arm previously mentioned to give extra control to the rear axle. The new suspension arrangement permitted a significant change in the front/rear brake balance, from 40:60 to 57:43.

There are some minor changes to the instru-

ments and controls. Perhaps the most significant change is that the gear and handbrake levers, while remaining on the right hand side, are each repositioned so as to be less in the way should the driver, perversely, decide to leave via the right hand door. The instrument layout is altered, with the speedometer and tachometer spaced symmetrically each side of the steering wheel, and the horn button is now a double-ended affair giving a choice of loud or soft. On the steering wheel boss there are now only two levers – ride control and hand throttle – as both the ignition timing and the starting mixture are controlled automatically. Finally, it was now possible to order an interior heater as a factory-fitted item.

Summing up, one could say that the Mark V was now all the things a Bentley should be. It had been given a strong, rigid chassis, it had independent front suspension, there was synchromesh on three of the four ratios, and it retained its excellent damping system. Equally importantly, it had a

The Mark V chassis. The additional bracing running forward from the line of the gearbox turns the front chassis members into virtual box sections.

B16AW was one of the few Mark V chassis which were completed and delivered, but not until July 1940 in this case. It is fitted with the standard Park Ward saloon body.

more robust crankshaft and there was hope that the big end and main bearing troubles were over. As to its weight, there had been close attention to keeping this down during the car's development, with comparisons between different prototype chassis and bodies and even with the Jaguar's weight breakdown. Ideally the objective was to get the new car down to below the 4¼ Litre, but this was always going to be an ambitious target. In the end Robotham was forced to confess that "we shall

be satisfied if the B.V. chassis starts off in production no heavier than the 'M' series Bentleys it replaces".

All that remained was to put the car into the hands of the motoring press in September, the month before the Motor Show. Unfortunately something else happened in the early days of September 1939, and any thought of a Motor Show had to be abandoned. As things turned out, virtually nothing was written up about the Mark V (or at least the standard version) until late 1940. Laurence Pomeroy Jr, Technical Editor of *The Motor*, had managed to get his hands on the London sales demonstrator – FYH539, a standard Park Ward four-door saloon on chassis B20AW which had formerly been experimental chassis 7-B-V. This was the car later used by Arthur Sidgreaves, Rolls-Royce managing director, as his personal transport for the duration of the war. At this period it was still possible to obtain petrol in reasonable amounts for so-called essential use, and Pomeroy and his testing team decided to write something which was less than a full road test report but which nevertheless looked at the car in some detail. Pictures of the car show how much Park Ward had cleaned up the design of their standard saloon, and how similar it is to the post-war Mark VI. It is clearly wider, especially at the back, and boot capacity appears to be larger. There are no running boards, and instead the sills are turned outwards to act as protection against mud splashes. There are also no bonnet louvres, and one can see that the side panels of the bonnet are removable.

The testers' first impressions emphasised how much more space there was in the car. "It is possible to sit five with reasonable comfort; there is a luggage locker of roomy proportions coupled with a platform-type back, and there is ample legroom, despite there being no wells in the floor. This is the more remarkable because the 10 feet 4 inches wheelbase is 2 inches shorter than the previous model". They decided to drive the car out of London and round a semi-rural route through the Home Counties. Part of the report is more concerned with where they are going to find a decent lunch, their first choice being "crowded with refugees, and we gathered that we should have booked at least three weeks before to have obtained any food". In between times, though, they marshalled their thoughts about the car. They had to admit first that it was by no means the fastest car they had ever tested, estimating its true maximum as about 85-90mph. "Some experienced motorists – particularly those who journey on the Continent – may consider it on the slow side", although Pomeroy failed to add that motoring in continental Europe had temporarily gone out of

Another of "the few" is chassis B20AW, also a standard Park Ward saloon, here shown in early wartime guise with a masked headlamp.

fashion. It would also seem that, despite comments on its "extremely rapid pick-up", its acceleration was in truth less rapid than might have been expected.

That apart, though, they found it "superlative" in every other respect. "There is no comparison between this car and the previous type. It is true that it retains all the virtues of the previous model, also that it avoids its few vices. In character, however, it is wholly changed and, in my view, it

Mark V – Summary Statistics

Engine

configuration	6 cylinders in line, overhead valves, pushrods
capacity	4257cc
bore	3½in (88.9mm)
stroke	4½in (114.3mm)
RAC rating	29.4hp
compression ratio	6.5:1
firing order	1 4 2 6 3 5
brake horsepower	125bhp @ 3800rpm
crankshaft:	
no of bearings	7
main bearing	2½in (63.5mm) diameter
big end	2in (51mm) diameter
cooling system	Water pump, in-line thermostat
ignition details	Coil, 12 volts, with automatic timing control
ignition timing	0-5° atdc [from Experimental dept files]
carburettors	Twin 1½in SU
fuel pump	SU double-capacity electric
dynamo and charging system	Rolls-Royce air-cooled, constant voltage control

Chassis

wheelbase	10ft 4in
track	4ft 8½in(front), 4ft 10in (rear)
length	15ft 11in
width	5ft 9in
weight	2719lb (1233kg)
turning circle	43ft right, 42ft 4in left
wheels and tyre size	16 x 6.50
steering box	Marles cam and roller
propellor shaft	Divided, centre bearing
rear axle	Fully floating on early cars, planned to be semi-floating, hypoid bevel
ratio	4.3:1
shock absorbers	Front: Armstrong hydraulic Rear: Rolls-Royce hydraulic with speed control and driver override facility

Gearbox

type	Four speed, synchromesh on upper three gears
gear ratios	3.59, 4.30, 6.15 and 10.5 to 1, reverse 10.4:1

Numbers Produced

35 chassis laid down; only 9 thought to survive

is the finest car for every-day motoring that it has been my pleasure to handle. In this seemingly extreme statement I am backed by my co-drivers." There were particular words of praise for the new independent front suspension, the damping, the "finger-light, beautifully accurate" steering, the new gearbox and the "magnificent" brakes. In this last area the testers immediately worked out what had changed: "there is no tendency for the rear wheels to lock, and evidently a large proportion of the braking is now taken on the front wheels". And they added "however hard the brakes are applied the steering is unaffected, and there is no tendency for the car to get out of control". Petrol consumption they estimated at between 16 and 20mpg.

This was not the end of the matter, however. In a later issue of the magazine Pomeroy found it necessary to correct the impression he had given of the car's performance. "I did not know when I put these thoughts into print that the car had been timed on the Continent to do close on 100mph. This figure seemed to indicate that all was not quite perfect with the car as originally tested. It later transpired that owing to the whole energies of the Derby factory being now concentrated on war work an error had crept into the carburetter setting which, although slight in itself, had made a very appreciable difference to the performance of the car." Pomeroy then had the opportunity to try our the car's performance again. "As compared with the data obtained on the previous run, it appeared as though we had either a new engine or a new speedometer. Ninety was readily obtainable on direct gear, to be comfortably maintained on the overdrive. The road was pleasantly free from traffic and, although not the semblance of a risk was taken nor was the Rolls-Royce servo called upon to exert full power on the Girling brakes, a highly satisfactory time was realized, showing that the gains in performance were real and not due to speedometer flatter [sic]."

During Pomeroy's second appraisal of the car he handed it over to another highly experienced motoring journalist, Gordon Wilkins, who added his own comments to Pomeroy's report. Wilkins was honest enough to admit some prejudice before he took the car over – "as for the previous 4¼ Litre Bentley, I was not one of its most fervent admirers" – so his subsequent praise is all the more convincing. He, too, was impressed with every aspect of the car: speed, suspension, steering, gearbox and so on. He reserved his greatest praise for the brakes, expressed in his usual hilarious

Above: *A side view of yet another standard Park Ward saloon - chassis B34AW - brings out the car's resemblance to the postwar Mark VI.*
Left: *James Young were one of a number of coachbuilders who made proposals for the streamlined "Corniche" version of the Mark V.* **This design could well have been intended for the 1939 Motor Show.**

manner. ". . . it is difficult not to use superlatives. I believe the braking on the Mark V Bentley is the best that has so far been achieved on a motorcar. It gives the utterly smooth and progressive retardation found in a first-class passenger lift. I had not consciously appraised the braking qualities until we surmounted a rise at about 80 and found the road blocked by a lorry passing some parked cars. This seemed a most suitable opportunity to use the brakes."

So once again the company's honour was satisfied, but only after they had protested. The truth is that there was inevitably some variation between one car and another.

The Experimental department was aware that the most efficient way by far of improving maximum speed was by reducing the car's air resistance. There had been continuing efforts in this direction over several years, as we shall see in the next chapter, but they all involved major changes to the frontal appearance of the car. This was completely acceptable to some, who really did want to cruise on Continental roads at high speed, and a total anathema to others who cherished the traditional radiator. If the war had not got in the way, we should have seen the company drawing the logical conclusion and producing two types of body for the two sorts of buyer. Of these, the standard Mark V saloon which Pomeroy tested was for the traditionalist, and alongside it at the 1940 Motor Show there would have been a quite different shape altogether – the Corniche.

Chapter Seven

The Late Experimental Cars

This is the story of two experimental cars – the "Paulin car" (sometimes known as the "Embiricos car") and the Corniche – which together had a profound effect on the company's thinking. Rolls-Royce had run experimental cars as a matter of course, whenever a new car was under development. They were modified as necessary to test new ideas as they came up during the test period. In a number of cases, and especially after the streamlining craze began in 1933, these ideas involved the aerodynamics of the car, and we have already seen some examples in previous chapters. This is a matter of bodywork design, and in the earlier years such work as there was concentrated on two areas – the tail of the car and the front wings. To begin with designers were obsessed with the idea of the so-called "true streamline" shape, which was envisaged as being similar to a teardrop. Thus whenever they were called upon to design a "streamlined" shape they began with a

The Paulin (or Embiricos) car. Note the parabolic front wings and enclosed rear wheels.

sloping tail. The minimum requirement was that the tail should slope when seen from the side, but preferably it should also taper at the sides as well, so as to approach more closely the teardrop shape.

In practice, as the Experimental department soon found out, while this style looked modern and progressive it did very little to reduce a car's air resistance (they used the term "windage"). What did make a difference was to "streamline" the front wings, in particular by bringing them forward and down so that they enclosed the wheels much more, and also by giving them a parabolic shape behind the wheel. Soon the testers were talking much more the language of the aerodynamicists, and references to a car's frontal area occur in the memos with increasing frequency. There was also a certain air of resignation, however, since they recognised that the typical tall, vertical radiator of the 1930s car – and few were taller than the Bentley or Rolls-Royce – was the main culprit in raising air resistance, along with headlamps, horns and other paraphernalia. Their resignation was founded in the belief that the only long-term solution was to place the engine at the rear, something which various pioneers of streamlining – men like Jaray and Rumpler – had been propounding since 1920 and earlier, but which resulted in cars of such an outlandish appearance that no-one would buy them.

At the same time the pressure to find more speed was relentless. Partly this was just competition in the golf club car park, but a new factor was the availability of purpose-built high speed roads in Germany and Italy, unlike in Britain where acceleration was the more useful quality. Thus the internal pressures, especially from the Sales department, on Hives and Robotham – and especially on the latter after Hives was promoted – were perpetually for more powerful engines. These two knew, however, that any increase in power had more effect on acceleration than on maximum speed (air resistance goes up not just with speed but with something between the square and the cube of speed), and that an improvement in the car's aerodynamics would be a much more efficient way of achieving the objective.

Incidentally, it is worth noting that many of the assumptions affecting developments in streamlining were later proved false. For example, droplets of liquid – be they water, tears or anything else – falling freely in air do not take up the elongated shape attributed to them; high-speed photography shows that, after breaking up into smaller drops, they assume a spherical form. Secondly, the aerofoil or tear-drop shape is inappropriate for an object such as a car moving close to the ground: there is no benefit in reduced drag by extending the tail to a point. (When Professor Kamm, working in Stuttgart in 1935, showed conclusively that this was so, the scientific community at first refused to believe him, and treated his results as a joke.) Thirdly, it is possible to reduce frontal drag without moving the engine to the rear of the car, as Chrysler in America and André Dubonnet in France were in the process of proving.

Chrysler, though, were part of the problem as well as of the solution. It was in 1934 that they had introduced their ground-breaking new model, the Airflow. The sensation of the New York Auto Show that year, it was the result of much wind-tunnel work, and it looked the part, especially with its dramatic curved radiator grille. Unfortunately its styling failed to win over the buying public – it was just too advanced for its time – and the design had to be rapidly softened for the next model year. This saga immediately became an awful warning to car manufacturers not to let innovation get too far ahead of public taste. The Rolls-Royce management were well aware of this lesson, and it meant that they were not in a hurry to solve their aerodynamic problems by streamlining the Bentley radiator.

A visit to Brooklands in April 1936 was something of a turning point for Hives and Robotham.

There they saw Dubonnet's streamlined car, and for a car which, as Hives put it in a report to Sidgreaves, was "made in a back yard", it made quite an impression on them. The engine was located at the rear, but within the wheelbase, and the driver sat virtually between the front wheels. "The effect of streamlining is the greatest point of interest about this car. It can do 109mph with 80 clutch bhp . . . Taking the results achieved by Dubonnet, it will be seen from the attached table that if Bentley windage could be reduced in the same manner, the result at 60mph on improved acceleration would be equal to reducing the car weight by over 9cwts." The remainder of the report makes it clear that Hives knows that a rear-engined car is out of the question, and that the answer to reducing air-resistance will involve a dramatic change in the shape of the radiator. "It is of course accepted that our clientele is probably the most conservative in the world, and for this reason our main concern at present is confined to knowing what other manufacturers are gaining from reduced windage, and whether there is any small modification that can be made to our products to improve their drag . . . Briefly, we are proposing to spend a small sum annually on wind tunnel work."

Even so it took more than a year before anything came of the proposal, and in August 1937 the Experimental department began to use the wind tunnels at the Bristol Aeroplane Company to test their body designs. At first they only managed to confirm their own gloomy opinions of the stan-

An overhead view of the Paulin car shows how the tail tapers in plan as well as in elevation.

This shot of the car's tail emphasises its sharp taper even more.

These two illustrations show the way in which even the door handles were "streamlined" by recessing them into the thickness of the door.

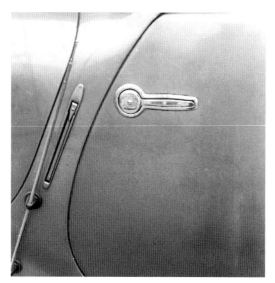

dard bodies, including demonstrating that the saloon would go some 15mph faster backwards than forwards under the same power. A test against an equivalent Oldsmobile, which was somewhat larger in frontal area, showed it to have 15% lower air resistance than the Bentley. Their next step should logically have been to test an experimental streamlined car, but since that would have to wait until British tastes had caught up there was little justification for building such a car just then. It was at this point that their thoughts turned to customers in continental Europe, who had more need for increased top speed and who had fewer inhibitions about sloping radiators. And the person they needed to turn this into reality was already involved in all the correspondence: Walter Sleator, Rolls-Royce's manager in Paris.

Sleator had a friend (and customer) in Paris who he thought might be just the person to be interested in a unique, trend-setting Bentley, and so it proved. This was André Embiricos, who duly ordered a car with a special streamlined body, subject to certain conditions. These were that the engine should produce 140bhp, that "adequate brakes should be fitted" (important where air resistance would have much less braking effect than normal) and that the gearing should be correct for the car's expected maximum speed (at that stage they were talking about a heady 123mph). Up to this point the car was being referred to as the "Vanvooren Bentley", Vanvooren being a distinguished firm of Paris coachbuilders who had already bodied a number of Bentley chassis. They had a reputation as innovators in both design and manufacturing methods, and it was understood that they would be the builders of M Embiricos's body.

The first step, however, was to agree drawings of the proposed design, before testing a scale model in the wind tunnel. Two different frontal treatments were offered, one with the headlamps in the wings and the other with them located in the wing valances, the second being the one chosen. Evernden and his colleagues were highly impressed with the way in which the design produced virtually as much seating room as the standard car, yet within the confines of a stream-lined exterior, and wanted to learn more about the person who was responsible. This turned out to be a M Paulin, whom Sleator described as an "aerodynamic engineer" (although he had actually trained as a dentist), and it was eventually decided that his name should be used as the name of the project.

Georges Paulin had already made his name by designing the streamlined Peugeot entrants for the 1937 Le Mans race, which had been the subject of much admiration. The wind tunnel tests, at Vickers this time, were very encouraging, and in fact the finished car was to bear a close resemblance to the scale model, right down to its rear wheel spats.

In January 1938 the experimenters had built a full-size wooden mock-up of the car and were finalising its specification. Certain changes were obvious, such as finding a new way of supporting the radiator (no bonnet stay), modifying the air cleaner (lower bonnet line) and using an in-line thermostat (no radiator shutters). However there were numerous other variations from standard specification, including a higher 8:1 compression engine, larger carburettors, aluminium front brake drums and a 12:41 (3.42:1) rear axle ratio as had been used for the abortive 1936 Le Mans attempt. It would appear that this very high ratio was chosen because the overdrive gearbox for the M-series cars was not yet ready. The quoted theoretical speed at the engine's 4500rpm limit was 115mph.

Despite the earlier involvement of Vanvooren, the body was actually built by the smaller Paris concern of Pourtout. All was explained in a letter from Sleator to Sidgreaves: "The coachbuilders who built this body are known by the name of Pourtout, and the only reason why the body was built there was because Monsieur Paulin lives almost next door to them, and as he only left the coachbuilders to go to bed, it was more convenient for him. In agreement with the latter, a repeat order would be executed by Vanvooren". The finished car, chassis B27LE, was ready for testing in July, so Robotham went over to Paris and took it to the Monthléry track. His high hopes of reaching 115mph were dashed, however, and the 104mph maximum that he actually achieved he put down to the car being over-geared. Nevertheless it had still managed to lap 15mph faster than the standard car, and overall Robotham was very pleased. He wrote to Hives: "It is the first really practical aero-dynamic car that I have tried. Its best feature is the way it handles. Sleator considers, and I agree with him, that it is more roadworthy than his normal demonstration car. It appears to be almost entirely unaffected by side winds."

It is worth stopping a moment to take in the scale of Paulin's achievement. He had produced a body which not only fulfilled the aerodynamic requirements but was also perfectly practical for everyday use. Interior seat width was equal to the

standard saloon's, although the car suffered from the usual two-door coupé's problems of limited height and access for the back seat passengers, and also restricted luggage space. Even its construction and detailing were the subject of admiring comments when the car was eventually brought to Derby for a short time. Not the least of Paulin's achievements (doubtless with the help of the Pourtout concern) was that he had kept the weight down to 31cwt (1575kg) compared with 34cwt (1730kg) for the standard saloon. As for the car's appearance, the perpetual problem was "Conduit Street", the London showroom, where the sales staff were faithful reflections of their customers' ultra-conservatism. They were recognised as the hardest nut to crack, but Robotham was prepared to have a try. "We heard nothing but

The tail of the Paulin car contained both the spare wheel and a reasonable amount of luggage space. Access to luggage was unusual but ingenious.

This side view of the Paulin car emphasises its sleek, wind-cheating shape.

In Germany, February 1939, on the way to the autobahn test.

praise for the appearance of the car. It would certainly create a great deal of interest if it were exhibited at either the [Paris] Salon or [London]. We consider that this car is a very useful piece of experimental apparatus and if, as we understand is possible, the customer would loan it to the company for a few weeks, we recommend that it is brought over to be examined by Conduit Street."

Such an excursion did in fact take place, in September, although it was a much curtailed visit because of the Munich crisis and its immediate aftermath. Nevertheless the car went to Conduit Street, and the reaction of the sales staff was predictable. Robotham, reporting on the trip to Sleator, was philosophical: "[Conduit Street] as one could have anticipated were not enthusiastic, but they will be educated." He then turned his mind as to how else he could exploit the use of the Paulin car, especially in the context of a publicity campaign to highlight the company's technology (to which reference has been made in an earlier

chapter). The Paulin car could, he proposed, make an observed high-speed run on a German autobahn, and also do a 12-hour or 24-hour run at Monthléry – both locations chosen, presumably, with the car's likely overseas buyers in mind. The car was prepared accordingly and tested in January at Monthléry. For some reason both 19-inch and 17-inch wheels were tried, but the gearing on the smaller tyres meant it was running continuously at 4500rpm, which inevitably resulted in a big end failing. It could well have been this which led to the decision to fit the overdrive gearbox from the then current M series cars, as by the beginning of the following month the overall gearing using overdrive was 2.87:1, still with the 3.42:1 axle ratio.

G E T Eyston had been lined up to carry out the Monthléry run, but for some reason Sleator himself carried it out, on 27 January 1939. In spite of there still being ice and snow on parts of the track, he covered 107.4 miles in one hour, with an additional last lap at 110mph. Fuel consumption was 12.25mpg, and oil temperature a worrying 103°C. Strangely, the company sat on this very fine achievement for a few weeks before releasing details to the press, perhaps not wanting to overshadow what was to come next. On 1 February, therefore, Sleator set out from the Paris showrooms with a party of journalists including John Dugdale of *The Autocar* who subsequently wrote up the trip. Robotham accompanied them driving a standard car (B6MR) which had a Vanvooren pillarless four-door saloon body. Crossing into Germany in the Saar, they joined the autobahn at Mannheim and went as far as Ulm before the ice and fog persuaded them to stop for the night. The next day they began the high speed test proper, and at one stage covered 24 miles in a quarter of an hour, a 96mph average , with a maximum recorded speed of 118mph. Estimated petrol consumption was 20mpg at 80mph and 17mpg at 90.

Dugdale's article, waxing lyrical about "a new form of motoring; it is the nearest thing to flying", duly appeared a couple of weeks later. The following week *The Motor* – exclusively – ran the story of Sleator's Monthléry achievement as if it had just happened. Later they ran a description of the Paulin car and a passing reference to the autobahn run. In such devious ways did the Rolls-Royce press office manage to keep both magazines happy. Interestingly, the two journals had been briefed to point out that the company would be happy to produce replicas of the Paulin car for any buyer who wanted one. "If anyone wishes to purchase today the car of tomorrow", trilled *The Motor*, "all he has to do is to square the bank manager and take a taxi to Conduit Street". Do we detect the mischievous hand of Robotham in that innocent phrasing?

The next piece of publicity was to be a one-hour run at Brooklands, but the decision was made to defer this until nearer the time of the Motor Show. Accordingly Eyston used the car for some testing at Brooklands in early March, which amongst other things were intended to solve the oil temperature problem. There was then a lull, but suddenly in July things started to happen, triggered by a rumour that Lagonda were preparing a similar test. Last-minute work included fitting Hartford shock absorbers (the ones from Eddie Hall's TT car) as the Brooklands track was notoriously bumpy. The run took place on 18 July, Eyston putting 42 laps into the hour and thus averaging 114.6mph. This was achieved in less than ideal conditions, since there was a strong wind during the test as well as light rain.

Immediately after the test Embiricos decided to sell the car, and it became the property of H S F Hay, in whose ownership the car achieved further fame by competing at Le Mans in 1949 and finishing sixth; he entered the car twice more, in 1950 and 1951. Although Conduit Street did in fact receive at least one order for a similar car no others were made, and B27LE remains a unique reminder of a fascinating period of Bentley history. Its main achievement was to have alerted the Rolls-Royce management to the possibility that such radical styling could still attract a certain type of buyer, and it led directly to the Corniche project.

It was becoming obvious during the last days of 1938 that the Mark V, due to be launched at the 1939 Motor Show, was not going to be much more of a performer than its predecessor the 4¼ Litre, and was likely to look rather slow compared with its key competitors. Accordingly a project was started under the name "Continental" to produce an alternative version of the Mark V. To be given the model name "Corniche", this would have an aerodynamic body based on the Paulin Bentley but adapted to provide four doors and increased passenger and luggage space. Additional emphasis was put on saving weight (but not, apparently, cost) in both the body and the chassis. The objective was to have at least one example at the Show in October, side by side with its more conventional sister.

A memo from Robotham to those involved sets out the very tight timetable to which the company

was committing itself. "For this [the Motor Show] to be achieved, we consider that the 15,000 miles' test in France should be completed by August 1st. Our records show that from the start of a test to the examination of a car can hardly be accomplished in less than two months. Therefore, the Continental car will have to be completed ready for test on May 30th. Vanvooren's say that they cannot get very far with the body unless they have the chassis on which to build it. A dummy chassis is no good because the wings, cowling, etc. become almost an integral part of the frame. We have, therefore, said that we will let them have the car in as complete a condition as soon as possible in order to let them get on with the body. Obviously there will be a number of special features which we shall not be able to finish in time, and it is proposed to bring the car back from France when the body is mounted to be brought up to date before it commences the test."

The timetable he set out gave 14 January as the

A standard "overdrive" 4¼ Litre, B6MR, with a Vanvooren pillarless saloon body accompanied the Paulin during its German trip.

At Mannheim, ready to join the autobahn for high-speed testing.

Proof! The speedometer reads 110mph, with the engine turning over at 3500rpm.

The Paulin car at Brooklands, July 1939, ready for the one-hour test run.

date when all chassis drawings would be available, while the completed chassis was to be handed over to the Experimental department (for despatch to France) on 19 February. To make matters worse, this was not just another Mark V prototype chassis but a totally revised design in an attempt to reduce weight wherever possible. The frame itself was of a thinner gauge steel than had been specified for the Mark V, magnesium alloy was substituted for steel in many of the castings, the rear axle was a lighter semi-floating type and steel road wheels were used instead of wires. Meanwhile M Paulin had been hard at work on the body drawings, the general concept of the design having been agreed between Evernden and himself, and these were due to be

handed to Vanvooren on 17 January. It would appear that the plan was initially to order two such bodies, so as to have one each with British and French instruments (and maybe left hand drive in the latter case) for exhibition at their respective Motor Shows. However this was soon increased to an additional six bodies, so that there would be cars available to sell soon after the shows. After some debate this order was placed with Vanvooren, on the basis that Park Ward were heavily involved with manufacturing Wraith bodies, and also that the then current rate of exchange would permit importation from France at a competitive price. However there is some evidence of an intention that Park Ward would build one body, and that Vanvooren sent a kit of parts for them to do so, although it was never in fact built.

It seems that slippage in the timetable started to occur early on. A letter from Paulin dated 20 March, asking for permission to delete the Silent-bloc body mountings, refers to the chassis "which has recently come over". Certainly Vanvooren missed the ambitious date of late April for the completed car to be returned to England, and it was not until early June that the car was back in Derby. It briefly went on display for the benefit of employees, who admired its modern aerodynamic lines, large luggage capacity and ease of entry thanks to its pillarless construction. Meanwhile it had been decided that the standard Mark V engine was not appropriate, and a tuned version was substituted. This had an increased compression ratio (7.5:1), larger inlet valves, increased diameter inlet pipes and carburettors and a dual exhaust system. As a result it produced some 142bhp against the standard engine's 125, and in expectation of a significant increase in maximum speed it was given a higher rear axle ratio of 3.73:1, the gearbox being otherwise standard.

The Continental/Corniche was now ready for its intensive testing programme. First was Brooklands, starting on 20 June, where the car soon impressed by lapping at 109mph. It is important to note, though, that this speed was only obtainable on Dunlop racing tyres, whereas the Avon road tyres only gave 102mph. The difference was due to the much higher power absorption of the latter, which the tester involved estimated to be around 38hp. Even so, Robotham was clearly pleased, and felt confident that a 115mph lap would be perfectly feasible before Motor Show time. The car then set out on 30 June for France, accompanied by Big Bertha, an experimental Rolls-Royce limousine with a straight-eight engine. Robotham and Sleator were in the party to begin with, although the test programme in total was under the supervision of Ivan Waller. For once the autobahns were not used, since a 100kph (62mph) limit was in force, and instead the group headed south for Italy and the autostradas. There they covered over 2000 miles of hard testing, which included diversions through Cortina and the Stelvio pass, and found they could reach a top speed of 110mph.

The tests were in general very encouraging but showed up two fundamental problems, neither of which was capable of being solved quickly. Firstly, in certain circumstances at high speed the car behaved in an unstable manner, and indeed some found it somewhat frightening. Many years later Waller described the symptoms thus: "The form it took . . . was that the car had two directions in which it would go straight, at a guess perhaps half a degree apart, and that it would shift on its own from one to the other. It would be stable in either of the two directions of travel, but it frightened the driver into trying to do something about it with the steering." There was some consternation amongst the test crew, and their first suggestion to Derby was to modify the steering geometry. Derby responded with the news that the new parts would take six weeks, and instead made the helpful suggestion to add 200lb (100kg) of weight to the car's roof, so as to induce roll oversteer and allow the anti-roll bar to apply compensating action.

Before they complied with this suggestion, the testers tried another change which appeared to solve the problem – an increase in rim width and tyre section. Two days later, though, they changed

Driver George Eyston (second left) discusses his 114mph average with W R Robotham (left – by then in charge of the Experimental department), J A V Watson (Wakefield oil representative) and Millard Buckley, Rolls-Royce publicity manager (right).

back to the narrower rims and found that the problem did not reappear. Gradually they realised that the instability only occurred in certain weather conditions, specifically when it was windy, and the true nature of the problem began to unfold. It was, of course, an aerodynamic phenomenon: in simple terms the lateral centre of pressure was too far forward, instead of being firmly behind the centre of gravity as it should be. Obviously this was inherent in the shape of the body, and it was not going to be altered overnight. With today's knowledge it might have been merely a question of adding a "spoiler" at some critical location on the body, but at that time normal cars were only just reaching speeds where aerodynamics became an

14-B-V, the one and only Corniche prototype. The influence of the original Paulin car is very evident.

14-B-V during its fateful Continental testing in July 1939, pictured somewhere in the Dolomites.

issue, and there was no readily available body of knowledge.

An even more important fault, because it directly affected safety, concerned tyres. Numerous tyre failures occurred during the high speed tests, and it was clear that the car only had to be driven for about fifteen miles at top speed for this to happen. Worse, the failure was potentially catastrophic, the tread often separating suddenly from the carcass with a resounding crack. This was shown to be due to the temperature of the adhesive rising to the point where the bond was no longer strong enough, and was of course directly related to the power being absorbed into the tyre as we have previously noted. Although conditions on the Italian autostrada in mid-summer were probably as adverse as the testers were likely to meet, it was still clear that the tyre manufacturers had some work to do before the car could go on sale. Robotham was confident that the solution would not take them long, and perhaps if the pressure from Rolls-Royce had been maintained that would indeed have been the case, but in fact the motoring world had to wait until the 1950s before a truly satisfactory high-speed tyre became available.

Before many more days had passed, however, worse was to happen. At the beginning of August the car was involved in an accident with a bus and had to go back to the test centre at Chateauroux for repairs. Then a few days later, on 8 August, there was a much more serious accident, with

tester Rose at the wheel. Ivan Waller, at a later date, wrote a clear but dramatic description: "Percy Rose was driving 14-B-V from Chateauroux towards Issoudun on a wet road (roads were very slippery when wet in those days) when a vehicle was driven out of a farm track on the SE side of the road. Percy applied his brakes, got into a skid, left the road on his right hand side, knocked down a tree, went nose first into a deep ditch, bounced out, rolled over left handed, and finished up on his right hand side with the back end towards the road, the underside of the car facing down the road in the direction of Issoudun, and the offside rear wheel against a tree, in which it had milled a large slot."

Thankfully the driver was unhurt, but the car was very seriously damaged. When it had been taken back to Chateauroux the workforce removed the body and sent the chassis back to Derby for repair. It was at this point that someone at Calais, no doubt acting in the company's best interests, persuaded the port officials to accept the car's "carnet" (the document which testified to its re-export and thus avoided any payment of duty) even though half of the car remained in France. This was to lead to complications later when the company tried to re-import the body on its own. Derby had hopes of repairing the chassis by the end of August, and meanwhile the body was being repaired at Chateauroux, Vanvooren being judged too busy with the four bodies already ordered. The

accident had thrown out of gear all the plans for the Paris and London Shows – "the Corniche was quite irreplaceable and the accident could not have happened at a more inopportune moment" – and Robotham decided in effect to abandon the testing programme until the Show period was over.

When the declaration of war came on 3 September, it was of course followed by the cancellation of both Shows. This took all the immediate pressure off both the testing programme and the building of six Corniche cars. Although it took some time for the news to filter through to Derby, Vanvooren took the decision to close down virtually straight away; the body parts they had already made were stored, inaccessible to anyone. That still left the kit of parts stored at Park Ward. It must be remembered that this was the period of the "phoney war", before the invasion of France, and in the correspondence of the time there was very much a feeling of business as usual. The company wanted to have at least two prototypes on the road, so there was some discussion as to whether Park Ward could body one of the four Corniche chassis available, perhaps with Paulin supervising. However Paulin was technically by now mobilised in the army although on indefinite leave, and could not leave France, so that scheme had to be dropped. Instead there were discussions – right up to May 1940 – about sending a chassis plus the crated body to the coachbuilder Kellner, where Paulin was now working, but evidently nothing came of this scheme either.

That still left the repaired prototype body to be reunited with one or other of the chassis. It was sent off to England via Dieppe, where it lingered at the dockside bogged down in paperwork. At one point the RAC representative appeared to be telling the company that the item could not exist, as the chassis on its own would not have been allowed to re-enter England without its body. The final wistful note, dated 29 May, makes it clear that any further thought of getting it back is out of the question, even in the unlikely event that it had not been destroyed by enemy action.

And that was the end of the Corniche project. Park Ward's kit of parts was destroyed when the Rolls-Royce Lillie Hall premises were bombed, and the four half-finished bodies stored at Vanvooren suffered a similar fate when that factory was bombed in 1943. Both Paulin and Jacques Kellner suffered for their British connections when they were found working for the Resistance and summarily shot. When Bentleys were made once more after the war they kept their traditional radiator, and the avant-garde frontal appearance of the Corniche was never seen again. Nevertheless one could say that the Corniche – always known internally as the "Continental" – was born again in 1952, when Bentley announced their super-fast, low-drag, Continental model. Maybe, even if the Corniche had gone on sale, this is the car into which it might have evolved.

The Bentley R Continental of 1952 – spiritual descendant of the Corniche?

Chapter Eight

On the Road Then

Typical owner-driver? 3½ Litre Mann Egerton saloon B63AE is pictured (we presume) with its first owner, Capt van Neck, Chief Constable of Norfolk.

The Derby Bentley was born at a fortunate time. Had its gestation taken only one year instead of two, it would have arrived into a world where Slump and Depression were words on everyone's lips, and where even those who still had money were anxious not to flaunt it. Indeed, part of the rationale for buying Bentley was to "get more chassis work into Derby", because sales of both Rolls-Royce models had been hit by the downturn in the economy. Car sales in general were down by some 15%, and for the top end of the market it was worse. 1931 and 1932 were the worst years, both for the market as a whole and for the 25hp segment, so just what sort of reception a new, flashy and very expensive sports car might have received in 1932 is open to question.

As it was, by the launch date of September 1933 there was a much more optimistic spirit through the country. Britain had just enjoyed an exceptionally good summer, and its economy was picking up well. Those who could afford an expensive car were no longer afraid of being conspicuous, and they flocked to see and buy the new "Rolls-Bentley". Perhaps the fact that it was almost a Rolls-Royce but not quite helped them make their decision; their friends could see that they were driving a product from the makers of "the best car in the world", but the radiator in front of them was not quite as ostentatious as that famous Greek temple. There is no doubt that at the time, at or near the top of the social scale, the Bentley rapidly became the car to be seen in. A quick perusal of the list of buyers confirms this: princes, dukes (royal and otherwise), maharajahs, earls, barons, film stars, captains of industry – their names litter the sales records throughout the 1930s.

This is not to imply that the Bentley was primarily a playboy's car, for the opposite was the case. The great majority of cars were bodied as saloons, and many of these were bought by sober, upright citizens who happened to be able to afford such a car. We should of course remind ourselves that there was a far greater differential in incomes in those days than exists now. The people who bought Bentleys then – men (almost always men) holding senior positions in industry, such as directors of large companies or chairmen of smaller ones – would have been earning, say, £4-5000pa upwards. Yet their employees working on the factory floor would have been lucky to earn £3 per week, or £150 per year. A differential such as this, some 40 times, was normal then but would be almost inconceivable today.

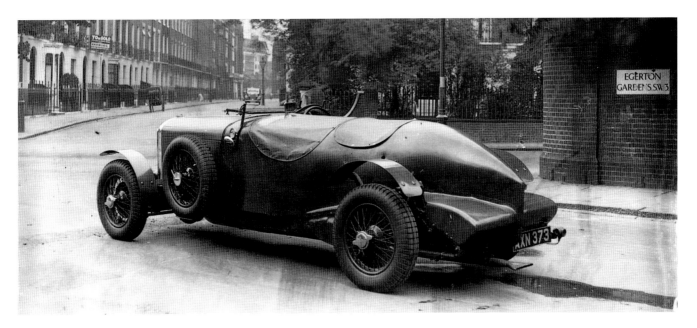

One assumes that anyone buying a Bentley was interested in driving, yet many owners would have employed a chauffeur for those occasions when it was inconvenient to drive themselves. It was the normal thing to do, just as one would have had a gardener and one or two domestic servants indoors; at the sort of wage rates we have been talking about it was an affordable cost. The sheer scale of domestic employment which existed in that era is something which one has to make an effort to imagine. Even as late as 1939 there were 2.3 million people employed in "personal service" in the United Kingdom, and the vast majority of these would have been in domestic service. Doubtless, though, even these owners took the wheel themselves when they could, so that they could enjoy the famed Bentley ride and roadholding.

For these buyers the "dual character" of the car would have been its main attraction. When they wanted to go shopping or to the theatre, being driven into town and dropped by the chauffeur, the car would have behaved like the town carriage that it was. Yet at other times, when the owner needed to get quickly to an appointment 50 miles away, the car's sporting side would come into its own and it would cover the ground as quickly as any rival. Increasingly, as the amount of traffic grew year by year, it would be acceleration rather than sheer top speed which would be the quality the driver appreciated most out of town. Most of this traffic would have been travelling at around 35-40mph, so the Bentley's ability to accelerate from, say, 40 to 70mph in around 12 seconds

would have been regarded as magical, enabling the car to overtake rapidly and then resume its cruising pace. That such speed differentials were the norm was confirmed by *The Motor*'s road test of an "overdrive" model in 1939, in the context of a mild complaint about the horn not having a strong enough note: ". . . at 80mph one is overtaking normal traffic at the rate of about 20 yards a second, so that to give even 10 secs.' warning the horn must have a penetrating note at a range of 200 yards." Implicit in this calculation is that the "normal" traffic being overtaken is travelling at about 40mph.

Britain's roads were already becoming the subject of comment. While the country's standard of living led to more and more of its citizens being able to afford a car, the roads remained largely unchanged. There were a number of bypass schemes to avoid the most congested town centres, but there was no programme to build special high-speed roads such as there was in Germany and Italy – and of course in the United States. Nevertheless to modern eyes British roads would have looked almost empty. *Motor Sport*, for example, taking a 4¼ Litre to Scotland for an extended test in 1938, encountered only a single car coming the other way during one-and-a-half hours' early morning motoring. Out of town there were still plenty of opportunities to reach a car's maximum speed, as Hives and Robotham did regularly on the Spondon bypass near Derby, for example, or on the A5 between Weedon and Towcester. The difference was that you could not

When Offord wanted to photograph their coachwork (such as on Eddie Hall's TT Bentley) they just rolled the car into the suburban London street - they knew there wouldn't be much traffic about.

A 4¼ Litre (chassis B100GA, a very early all-steel saloon) enjoys a spot of rural testing in 1937. Note the state of the road surface.

The same 4¼ Litre in the Shropshire town of Bridgnorth. The lack of traffic is astounding to modern eyes.

hold these speeds for any length of time, so the oil film on the big end or main bearings was not under stress long enough to break down.

It was a different matter if you took the car to the Continent. Many higher-income owners began to indulge in foreign touring holidays in the 1930s, if only to escape the drivers of Austins, Fords and Morrises who were doing exactly the same thing in England. The favourable exchange rates were also a factor, it must be said. It was Continental touring as much as anything which forced coachbuilders to increase luggage capacity so significantly. Whereas at the beginning of the decade it was acceptable to strap a cabin trunk on to the luggage grid, a few years later there had to be a luggage boot which would take at least a couple of cases, and which could be extended by folding down the lid to make a platform. Even this was soon unacceptable – the boot then had to take three or four cases with the lid shut and locked. These trends can be traced faithfully in the successive body styles offered on Bentleys during the period. The prevalence of punctures on Continental roads was also an influence, giving rise to a fashion for two spare wheels – either on the back of the luggage trunk or, later, mounted symmetrically in the valances of the front wings.

Then, after the car had been swung on to the ship at Newhaven and swung off at Dieppe, the long, straight Continental roads beckoned. Forget for a moment the autobahn and the autostrada – even the French routes nationales could support sustained high speed for much longer than was possible in England. They were straighter, and the population density was lower, as was car ownership. Here was an opportunity to find out just what the Bentley would do, and here also more than one car came to grief with bearing or crankshaft damage. It was this sort of experience, coupled with test results, which led to the infamous warning to customers not to exceed 4500rpm. But it was in Continental conditions, too, that the painstaking Rolls-Royce testing programme bore fruit, so that the lower gears were just right for storming Alpine passes, for example, and the steering lock was sufficient for the hairpin bends. And if one were to do the same thing in winter time, when it was normal to put snow chains on the tyres for extra grip, one could be certain that these had been tested too, and that there was sufficient room for them within the wheel arches (although you were specifically warned not to put one on the offside front tyre, as it would foul on full lock!).

The prospect of Continental touring will have been a strong influence on many buyers' choice of coachwork. This must have been one of the most pleasurable aspects of buying a Bentley, particularly – dare one say – for the female half of a partnership. Although there were many near-standard designs of body for the car, none of them came with the chassis when it left the Derby works. The availability of standard designs was undoubtedly a help to the Bentley salesmen, since they were able to quote a fixed price from a catalogue rather than wait for the coachbuilder to quote. It helped in other ways, too, firstly by allowing the coachbuilder to plan some batch production and bring his prices down, and also by encouraging the dealers to place orders for stock. So even if our buyer and his lady were looking to buy one of the standard designs, they had plenty to choose from and could often see finished examples in the showroom.

If they wanted to be a little more daring and commission a unique design, the choice was almost infinite. There is no doubt that the Bentley chassis was the mainstay of the coachbuilding business in the latter 1930s, with some 60 firms known to have built bodies for it, over 40 of them British. Some of these – some of the 22 who only built one Derby Bentley body – were small provincial firms whose coachbuilding departments were on their last legs but who had always had a relationship with the buyer's family. By contrast, Park Ward (helped by their close relationship with Rolls-

Continental touring - a typical French road in the winter of 1939.

A later 4¼ Litre, chassis B119JY, in a typical rural setting while on test in late 1937.

The lady in the 1938 Gurney Nutting sedanca coupé (chassis B124LS) is one of many who chose an open car during that year's hot summer.

Another 4¼ Litre drophead in 1938, this time an overdrive model by Vanden Plas on chassis B4MR.

Royce) built getting on for half of all the Derby Bentley bodies, and five times more than the next two most prolific firms, Thrupp & Maberly and Vanden Plas. Nevertheless our buying couple were free to order their coachwork from whoever they pleased – provided that the firm was a Rolls-Royce approved supplier, that the finished body was within the stipulated maximum weight, and that the body passed the company's final inspection.

The main choice buyers had to make was between a closed and an open car. This might seem surprising, given that by the mid-1930s the vast majority of new cars were saloons, and only some five per cent were open models. However this was a reflection of the success of the small all-steel saloon such as the Austin Seven, Ford Eight

and Morris Eight, where high volumes of steel pressings had brought down prices of such cars to near the £100 mark. Their open versions, by contrast, were significantly more expensive – between 25% and 50% more in some cases – and unsurprisingly only sold in small numbers. With a coachbuilt body, however, these differentials did not apply; indeed the cheapest Bentley standard body was the Vanden Plas open tourer. More importantly, a drophead coupé cost virtually the same as a saloon, so the decision was not a matter of price.

Thus it is not so surprising to learn that open versions of the Derby Bentley accounted for nearly one quarter of all bodies made. Of these the great majority were drophead coupés, so the popularity

of this style at the time is clear. Why this should have been so is less easy to pinpoint, but the attraction of having an open car on a Continental touring holiday must have been at least partially responsible. Even touring in Britain had its appeal, particularly during the good summers of 1933 and 1938. By this stage of its development, too, the drophead coupé style had eliminated most of its former disadvantages. It was during this period that the type variously known as sedanca coupé, coupé de ville or three-position drophead coupé became popular. Here the forward part of the hood can be folded back separately, leaving a sort of halfway house between open and closed and – perhaps more importantly – needing less time to close the car when rain arrives. There must always be some compromise on space in a drophead coupé since the hood takes up room when it is folded, but designers had managed to minimise this intrusion so that both passenger and luggage

space were still acceptable. That apart, a coach-built drophead coupé was finished to just the same high standard as a saloon.

There was another reason for some buyers to want an open car, and that was the strange matter of driving in fog. Such an attitude went back to the dawn of motoring, and enshrined a preference to be out in the open when fog was about, so that one could both see and hear to the maximum. We have to remember, too, that at least in cities and major towns fogs were simply thicker in those days, before the Clean Air Acts had done away with coal fires in every house. To these drivers the only way to continue was to put the hood down, and preferably the windscreen too if possible. Even saloon car drivers had the same feeling, which is why the opening windscreen was perpetuated on British saloons long after Continental countries had dropped it and fitted vee windscreens instead.

A 4¼ Litre overdrive Park Ward saloon, chassis B82MR, enjoys the seaside air in early 1939.

Alvis were a constant competitor to the Bentley during the 1930s. This is a 1937 Speed 25 four-door tourer with coachwork by Cross & Ellis.

Another reason for the need to open hoods, or windscreens, or at least a window, was the matter of demisting. Only after the motor industry had converted most buyers to the advantages of the saloon style, with its lack of draughts, did it realise that it had a problem with windscreens and windows misting up. To some extent this was alleviated by the system of quarter lights front and back, but these were less than fully effective on the windscreen. Before pressurised ventilation and demisting systems were introduced, some coach-builders even went to the extent of fitting additional windscreen wipers inside the glass, usually cleverly concealed behind the dashboard when not in use. The lack of built-in heaters also meant that it was normal to drive or ride in a car dressed in a thick overcoat plus scarf and gloves, not to mention the obligatory hat.

One comfort which began to appear regularly in cars of the Bentley class as the decade progressed was a radio. Although reception under the medium or long wave "amplitude modulated" regime of the time was inferior to today's "frequency modulated" system, radio technology had already come a long way from when the aerial had to be nearly as big as the car. By the mid-1930s aerials were being neatly fitted at the side of the scuttle or even under the running board, with apparently satisfactory results. As the price of fitting a radio came down, more and more cars were designed from the outset to allow easy installation. At the 1938 Motor Show it became the norm for a limousine to have a radio fitted in the rear compartment, although it would be much longer before the chauffeur was deemed worthy of having a set of his own.

Needless to say not everyone who aspired to a Bentley could afford a brand new example, and there was a thriving secondhand market. The Bentley was particularly attractive as a used car, since its Rolls-Royce credentials meant that one could have confidence in its durability, as well as it having been properly maintained. In December 1935 *The Autocar* tested a used 3½ Litre, with H J Mulliner saloon bodywork which had been first registered in May the previous year, and found it to be in as near new condition as made no difference. It had covered 10,800 miles and had obviously loosened up nicely, since when they tested the performance at Brooklands they produced acceleration figures which were a distinct improvement on those of a new car. Its maximum speed, too, might well have been an improvement had the conditions not been wet and windy. The history of the car, which we can pick up from the archives, is

Lagonda were perhaps the closest competitor of all, particularly after their 1935 reorganisation. This is the V12 drophead coupé.

Talbot were another marque competing for the customer's favour. Here is their 3½ Litre Airline saloon of 1935.

significant in itself. It had been purchased new in 1934 by the Hon Alexander Shaw, a director of the Bank of England, and he had relinquished it – presumably traded it in – in favour of an apparently identical H J Mulliner saloon in August 1935. This habit of changing one's car every year was not uncommon amongst the classes who could afford to do so, but the fact that Mr Shaw decided to stick to the Bentley marque is a decided compliment.

The asking price for the used Bentley was £1100, compared with £1585 new, so it probably cost Paddon Bros (the dealers offering the car for sale) about £900. A depreciation of over 40% in fifteen months looks steep to our eyes, but it was the norm at a time when cars simply did not hold together so well. This particular car, and many others like it, had probably been chauffeur driven for most of the time, which would suggest that it had been carefully run in and well maintained thereafter. Assuming that the new buyer kept it for, say, two years, he probably had a much better deal than Mr Shaw – but then somebody like Mr Shaw could afford it.

Assuming that our mythical buyers, whether seeking a new or a used car, had settled on a Bentley, what other makes might they have considered along the way? Possibles could have included such names as Talbot, Invicta (in the early years), Railton (later) or Jaguar (much later). Near-certainties would have been two marques, Alvis and Lagonda. We know that the Rolls-Royce management looked to these two manufacturers time and time again when comparing the Bentley with its competition. But it is clear that the car-buying public also used these two as benchmarks when assessing the Bentley. A perfect piece of evidence comes from "Contact's" gossip column in *The Motor* in May 1936, entitled "Delicate Ground":

"Still continuing to tread on very delicate ground, I am seeking to thrust upon you my impressions of three very notable British cars: in alphabetical order, Alvis, Bentley and Lagonda. All three are fine examples of the best traditions of British automobile engineering, and each is capable of a maximum speed exceeding 90mph. They have other things in common, such as driver-controlled shock-absorbers, six-cylinder push-rod ohv. engines, four-speed gear-boxes and good driving positions. After that you begin to find differences, as you will appreciate when you meet their respective owners.

"Playing for safety, I still continue to adhere to an alphabetical order. The Alvis appeals because of its low build, an excellent combination of accurate steering and road holding with independent front springing in the 3½ Litre and Speed Twenty models, while the all-synchromesh gearbox is another distinctive feature. The 3½ and 4¼ Litre Bentleys score on their almost supernatural silence and the high degree of refinement throughout the chassis. Everything works very smoothly, while third and top gears are extremely quiet.

"Finally, we come to the 4½ Litre Lagonda, as redesigned by Mr. W. O. Bentley, the outstanding feature of which is a powerful engine, turning slowly, with high top and third gears, which gives an effortless feeling when cruising fast. Not only can it go very quickly, but the efficient Girling brakes are a revelation in stopping. And it has a 10-ft. 9-in. wheel base. So there you have the three outstanding British makes which are competing for the favour of those who appreciate real motorcars regardless of cost. It is not for me to shatter illusions or seek further trouble this week by suggesting which is the best; the owners of the other two might disagree."

What we learn from this piece is not which of the three makes a motoring journalist would prefer (although one suspects the Bentley, if only for its "supernatural silence" and refinement) but that it was these three which were generally regarded as competing against each other. In terms of performance there was little to choose between them. As to price, whereas the differential was significant in the early years of the decade, with the Bentley much the most expensive of the three, it was steadily reduced as time went on, to the point where the V12 Lagonda's price was close to the Bentley's, while the Alvis – especially with one of the more exotic bodies – was not so far behind.

Another contemporary piece, in a publication called *Night and Day* in 1937, compared the Bentley against an Alvis 4.3. Both had Vanden Plas coachwork, the Bentley's being the drophead coupé version at £1550 while the Alvis was a £1185 pillarless saloon. In a refreshing contrast to the super-sensitivity shown by "Contact" in his piece in *The Motor*, this journalist was at least prepared to come out with his own opinions. It is evident from the start where his preference lies, if only because he devotes more than three-quarters of his space to the Bentley. He first lays down his requirements for cars in this class – "the top of the motoring tree" as he describes it. "It should be able to travel at 90 miles an hour, to accelerate from rest to 50mph through the gears in under 11 seconds, its

brakes should be 100 per cent efficient (which means stopping in 30 feet from 30mph), it should be able to hold the road like a leech, to travel in the Mall easily and comfortably yet be able to corner at speed, it should be moderately silent and not wildly expensive to run."

Given these criteria, he cannot find a word to say against the Bentley. As with many other testers before him, his overriding impression is the feel of the controls. "The most interesting thing about the car, both when you first take control of it and after several hundred miles, is the extraordinary ease with which you can drive it. Everything is exactly where it should be, the pedals are all well placed and the right height (a great rarity) and the controls work simply and well." As to the performance, he describes it as excellent but not surprising. "What is surprising is the way it goes about its work, without fuss or effort, almost without appearing to try... A speed of 70 to 75 seems to be the pleasantest for cruising and I should like to emphasise that at that speed, with its really good steering and superb brakes, it is a very much safer vehicle than the average baby car trav-

elling at 37 miles per hour." No doubt today's safety campaigners would disagree with the last sentiment, but readers at the time would have understood perfectly.

As to the Alvis, although it had "tremendous zest" it did not come up to the Bentley's standards in other respects. The engine was a little rougher, the springing was harder, it was less docile at low speeds and "less unobtrusive when being driven in the park". Overall it was judged to be "more of an enthusiast's car", which in this particular context was clearly not meant to be a compliment. Here, therefore, we have a journalist starting to articulate what people really felt about the Bentley compared with a formidable competitor. It was not being judged as a sports car at all, but was perceived as much more of an all-rounder, albeit one where in this highest class the performance of a sports car was taken for granted. When we couple this quality with the refinement of its controls and its silent running, we are at last getting to the heart of its appeal – at last beginning to understand how the most expensive car in its class could still outsell all its competitors.

By 1938 Rolls-Royce recognised the Jaguar 3½-litre saloon as a formidable competitor to the Bentley, bearing in mind its much lower price.

Chapter Nine

On the Road Now

If you are seriously contemplating the purchase of a Derby Bentley you will already have been looking at the classified advertisements to check prices and availability, and you will probably have been pleasantly surprised at both. Of the 2400 or so cars produced, a remarkable 70% per cent – say, 1700 – are estimated to survive, which means that there are always plenty of cars to choose from. It also means that prices will never achieve the rarity value of some particular models, and from most points of view this is all to the good; this book is not addressed to the sort of buyer who is interested in a car only as a speculation. It is to be hoped, too, that if you have not already joined one of the two clubs looking after the marque (more of this later) you are about to do so, as – amongst many other advantages – you will receive their advertising circulars, where members tend to advertise their cars first.

Once you start looking at particular cars you will probably be struck by the high standard to which they are maintained, probably higher than many other makes of "classic" car. There are several reasons for this. Firstly, even in the gloomiest period during the 1950s, when the preservation movement hardly existed and old cars were just a means of transport for impecunious students, Derby Bentleys often escaped the worst treatment. In this respect their Rolls-Royce heritage paid off, because the reputation of both these marques – not always justified – for high costs of repairs and spare parts frightened off the student brigade. More than that, though, Derby Bentleys

were sufficiently new by the start of World War Two to be still in the hands of people who could look after them properly, and as a consequence they emerged from their garages in 1945 in a much better state than most cars.

Yet another reason for the high standard of maintenance and preservation in which we find the cars nowadays is their sheer quality of engineering. They were designed and built to very high standards, and this has rubbed off on the sort of firm which specialises in the marque. In today's climate there are many specialists looking after the various makes of classic car, and they are all highly competent, but it was not always like that. Let us just say that, in the case of the Bentley, there is less likelihood that a car has been "butchered" at some period in its life. As for today, the owner of a Derby Bentley can be confident that firms specialising in the marque will be experts in every aspect of the car's specification, and that any work they carry out will be of a comparable standard to that when it was first built.

As to which model to buy, this will be very much a matter of personal choice. Some might say that the very early 3½ Litre cars are less attractive because they lack the more sophisticated speed-dependent damping system which also has the manual "ride control". On the other hand it is also true to say that these cars are as a result both lighter and less complicated to maintain. The 4¼ Litre cars are more powerful, but this is usually cancelled out by their having heavier bodies. The Mark V, of course, will feel more modern on the

road with its independent front suspension, but only a tiny number exist and they very rarely come on the market.

A more fundamental question, though, is the type of coachwork you are seeking: closed or open, saloon or drophead or tourer. It is always tempting to choose an open model, since we all have a dream of touring the countryside with the sun beating down on us. The reality, though, certainly in Britain, is that such days are far from guaranteed, and it is when the rain is beating down instead that we might be glad that we chose that comfortable, spacious saloon. Because the open cars are more sought after, they command higher prices, which is another way of saying that the saloons are more of a bargain. The only reservation with saloons concerns their coachwork, and it is even more necessary in this case to make sure that the frame is sound – not cracked or rotten (if it is wood) or not rusting (if it is a Park Ward steel frame). Removing panels to get at the frame for repairs is always expensive, but it is even more so with a saloon. Cracks around the windscreen pillars are a sure sign of trouble, and stains on the head-lining inside the rear window are nearly as bad.

If you still want to go for an open car, you have

to choose between a drophead coupé and a tourer. This is mainly a matter of comfort versus speed (or the impression of speed). A drophead coupé has wind-up windows, and usually its hood is lined, sometimes even padded. A tourer is essentially a sports car, and its weather protection is more limited – separate sidescreens, which have to be taken out and fixed to the doors or sides, and a more minimalist hood. If you want to be able to shut the car up at the first sight of rain, then it must be a drophead. If, however, the whole point of buying the car is to feel the wind in your hair, then look at a tourer. You must also consider your back seat passengers, if you intend to have any. With a tourer they are likely to be sitting quite high and a long way back from the screen, so at any reason-able speed they risk getting cold. On the other hand they will get a much better view of the coun-tryside than in a drophead coupé, since when the hood is up the people in the back seat see very little at all.

In all probability your final choice will be swayed by the lines of a particular car, and maybe by its colour as well. All the "standard" bodies built on Derby chassis were attractive, but there were also some dramatically beautiful special designs,

Derby Bentleys have often been campaigned in the milder forms of motor sport. Here a 1934 3½ Litre, B12AH, is seen competing at Prescott hill climb in the 1960s.

Some more enthusiastic driving in a 4¼ Litre Park Ward saloon, B133LE, at the Vintage Sports Car Club's Enstone driving tests in the 1970s.

many of which survive today. Whatever attracts you, make sure that you are not judging the car merely on the state of its bodywork, and that you investigate its mechanical aspects at least as thoroughly. It is hard to generalise as to which of the two is likely to cost more to bring up to standard, but if the bodywork is scruffy you can at least use the car, whereas if there are problems in the chassis or engine then you have to get them fixed before you can even get on the road. You will no doubt take expert advice on the mechanical condition of any car you are considering buying, but there are certain fundamentals which you can observe for yourself.

The easiest clue is of course oil pressure. After hitting a very high reading when the engine is started from cold, once the engine is fully warmed up it should manage around 20psi at 2000rpm, and 7psi at tickover. If the tickover figure is less than, say, 5psi this is not disastrous, but it does suggest that the pump needs looking at. Another point to look out for is noise from the crankshaft damper, which usually shows itself as a light buzzing – or sometimes much worse – when the engine speed goes through the 2300-2500rpm range. The cure is an overhaul of the damper including checking its torque setting, which means the radiator and the front of the engine coming off. Any other worries will depend on what you know of the engine's history. If there is any doubt about how recently it has been serviced, or even used, then you should at minimum have what Rolls-Royce used to term a "bottom end decoke", which involves dropping the

sump and cleaning out the oilways and sludge traps in the crankshaft. Thereafter the recommended procedure is to make several oil changes at 500-mile intervals and then use a modern multigrade oil, the detergent properties of which will keep everything clean. However at the same time you should fit a modern full-flow filter, if there is not one already; although this will technically make your car less original, it is generally accepted these days as a sensible modification.

Should you suspect that the engine has had a hard life or has not had a full overhaul for a long time, you may decide that it needs an expert to look at it more closely. One clue, for example, is that the bearing shells may have become loose in their housings, which happens after very long use because the Halls metal in the bearing gradually flows under compressive stress. In this case a complete stripdown of the engine is indicated, which will then also permit a detailed inspection of the crankshaft. If the slightest fault is found here – particularly any suggestion of a crack – then you should face up to the cost of a new crankshaft, since the risk of keeping the old one is too great and in any case the engine is already dismantled.

If at all possible you will want to give your proposed purchase a test drive. This is usually no problem if you are buying from a dealer, but if it is a private sale you must arrange to be insured. For preference you should begin the test with a cold engine so that you can see how easily it starts. This may involve using the starting handle, in which case you will have to disconnect the radiator shutter mechanism so that you can open the shutters to insert the handle. Remember also to set the ignition control to full retard. At an early stage in the test it is advisable to check two crucial elements – brakes and steering. The brakes should pull the car up perfectly evenly, and if they do not it means that one or other of the equalisers is not functioning. This in itself is a sign that the car has not been attended to recently and means that the offending component – a kind of miniature differential – probably has its gears blocked with old grease. Do not forget to check the handbrake as well, which has its own equaliser. Brakes can also develop problems at the front where the operating spindles pass through the front axle; a build up of rust at this point can again lead to uneven braking, or to a jammed return spring. If you can, try an emergency stop; the result should be two black lines from the rear wheels only, since once they lock the servo ceases to function, making it impossible to lock the fronts.

As to the steering, if there is a fault it is likely to show up in "stickiness" when on lock. This is particularly so with the 3½ Litre and early 4¼ Litre models, which use Rolls-Royce's own steering box (overdrive and Mark V models have the Marles box). This is a worm and nut design, with the nut lined with white metal, and although it will have worked perfectly when it left the factory, experience has shown that when the white metal wears it can lead to increased friction between the two surfaces. However you should only suspect the steering box once you are satisfied that the remainder of the steering components, particularly the kingpins, are in a satisfactory state. If the box is faulty, it can be restored.

During the test keep an eye on the temperature gauge; any suggestion of the radiator shutters (or the thermostat in the case of overdrive or Mark V models) not functioning properly will show up here. Another cooling system problem, which may or may not show itself during such a test, can occur with engines which have lain unused for some time. Here the suspended solids in the coolant can solidify in the water passages, and shifting them can be a long and tedious operation which can even involve stripping the engine. Listen for any noise from the rear axle, since wear in the pinion bearing can quickly lead to worn gear teeth as well, and that means an axle rebuild. The pinion should have no end-float at all, and this is something worth checking not only before purchase but every 12 months or so thereafter as

well. Early half shafts were weak, but most cars by now have the revised design from which the crucial stress-raiser has been eliminated. The half-shaft splines and those of the hub are joined by a driving dog, and this can often give rise to a clicking sound, indicating that the hub splines have worn.

The gearbox is a strong one and does not have a reputation for giving trouble, but first gear has straight cut teeth and can sometimes become noisy, as can the third/fourth gear synchromesh hub. However any noise in the gearbox is most likely to be a bearing, and replacements for these are available. Check the clutch for judder, particularly if the car is a 3½ Litre with the Rolls-Royce clutch. This has a centreplate which is susceptible

The Vanden Plas tourer is the ideal car for "wiggle-woggle" tests. Here 3½ Litre B15BN is taking part at Brooklands.

When using the starting handle on a cold engine, you must withdraw the pin in the radiator shutter mechanism so that you can open the shutters manually.

to heat distortion if slipped too much, whereas the later Borg & Beck design used on the 4¼ Litre is notably stronger. The recommended driving technique with the earlier clutch is to start off with the engine at tickover speed only, so that the clutch can be fully engaged almost instantly with minimum slip.

If you have the opportunity, it would be a good idea to test the ride control facility on the shock absorbers. This is fitted to all cars except the very early 3½ Litres (up to CR series chassis numbers), and is actuated by a lever on the steering wheel boss. If you cannot detect any change in damping effect, do not immediately blame the shock absorbers, as the fault could lie in the springs – or rather in their lack of lubrication. All four springs are fed oil from the Bijur "one-shot" centralised lubrication system, which is mounted on the scuttle and actuated by a foot pedal under the dashboard. Oil is fed under pressure to, amongst other places, the top four leaves of each spring, and spreads throughout the length of the leaf along herring-bone grooves cut in the top. The remaining leaves receive their oil by virtue of the whole spring being encased in a leather gaiter. If, as often happens, the lubrication system has become clogged with dirt, the spring leaves will no longer slide over each other easily and will start to act as additional dampers, with disastrous effects on the car's ride and handling. At the same time check that the one-shot system is delivering oil to all the other places that the makers intended. If it is not, resist the temptation to replace it with grease nipples (you will soon regret the extra work to which you have committed yourself) and instead bring the system back to working order; replacement parts are available.

If you had not driven a Derby Bentley before, your test drive should have persuaded you just how easy these machines are to drive. Although there is no synchromesh on first and second gears, there is sufficient torque for starting in second to be a normal procedure, after which the two remaining upward changes both have the benefit of synchromesh. A downward change into second gear, for example, will require the double-declutch technique, but this is not difficult and the gearbox is forgiving in this respect. Steering is – or should be – light and accurate, and the servo-assisted brakes are powerful by all but the most modern standards. Width judgment is easy, thanks to the high wings with their sidelamps visible on top, but reversing in a closed car shows up the lack of rear-

ward visibility compared with a modern car and initially you may well prefer to have some outside help. Once you start using the car, it will not be long before you are happy to take it anywhere, from short shopping trips to long cross-country journeys.

With high-performance cars of this era there is rarely any embarrassment with other road users. Naturally, 70 years of progress means that the modern car has caught up with the Derby Bentley's performance, but there are still some new cars on the market to which it can show a clean exhaust pipe. In practice you will be able to keep up with modern traffic with little difficulty. This is not an unimportant point, as it is in all our interests not to cause aggravation by driving too slowly and causing exasperation in the queue of traffic behind. There are enough pressures already on the old car movement, brought about by well-meaning legislators who fail to appreciate the importance of preserving our industrial history, and we should avoid at all costs giving them more ammunition.

As to the fuels available today, leaded petrol is only sold in a restricted number of outlets, and it is impossible to plan a journey of any distance using this fuel only. There is a certain risk, though, in using unleaded petrol, as it lacks the tetraethyl lead content which protects the valve seats from excessive wear. The alternative is to use normal unleaded petrol together with one or other of the additives now sold for this purpose, and this is the solution which most users have adopted. It is perfectly feasible to modify the cylinder head by adding hardened inserts for the valve seats, but this is an expensive operation and is probably best done when the head has to be removed anyway for other reasons. Current thinking is that valve seat recession is in any case a negligible factor with lower engine speeds (say, 3000rpm or below) and with engines such as the Bentley's which run at relatively cool temperatures. The acid test is how often you have to reset the tappets; only if the gaps seem to be closing up too quickly is there any need to suspect a problem.

Once you can take journeys in your home country in your stride, it may be time to consider travelling abroad. For those resident in the British Isles, this means touring in continental Europe, and few more pleasurable activities in old cars have yet been devised. Not only is there the promise of sunny days in unending succession, but the population and car densities are a revelation to those of us who habitually fight British traffic conditions. Touring in, say, France on minor roads – either the narrow red ones on the Michelin map or, even better, the yellow ones – is usually a close approximation to the conditions which must have prevailed in Britain in the mid-1930s. Any misguided Frenchman who is intent on getting somewhere quickly is soon seduced on to the autoroutes or routes nationales, leaving the minor roads for those whose journeys are concerned with the important things in life such as buying the ingredients for tonight's meal – not to mention stopping along the way for an aperitif and a chat. The same sorts of conditions apply in the right places in many other countries – Spain, Italy, Germany, the Scandinavian countries, to mention just a few.

Touring these areas in your pre-war car during the summer is relaxing and at the same time an adventure. Of course you will want to be sensible about it and make sure that your car is in tip-top condition before you set off, and you will have to check that your insurance is valid for the proposed trip. You would also be well advised to take a set of the crucial spare parts with you, and unless you have already learned what these are you should take the advice of your chosen specialist as to what should go into the kit. However the days of leaving your immobile car behind for three weeks while a new back axle is sent by sea are long over. These days there are fast, reliable courier services covering the whole of Europe, so if you have not brought the critical spare with you it should be possible to have it in your hands within a day or two. Furthermore the cost of a "get you home" insurance is small compared with the total cost of the holiday, and you can then travel secure in the knowledge that, if the worst happens, your precious vehicle can go home immediately on the back of a lorry. Some of these policies are better than others, especially where older vehicles are concerned, so it is worth shopping around – including through your car club – to find the best one.

Many drivers are understandably concerned about possible damage to their expensive old cars, particularly when they have to leave them unguarded either in their home country or abroad. Although there is always the possibility of vandalism, or – worse – theft, in practice it happens very rarely. Mainly this is because potential thieves recognise that such a car would be very difficult to sell on, since word of the loss would

soon get around the marketplace. Naturally it pays to take sensible precautions, ideally by leaving your car under a watchful eye, but if not then by at least removing the radiator mascot. Instead of leaving an untidy hole, you should obtain a "town cap" – ie a cap without a mascot, an item which is readily available. Incidentally, if you have become the owner of an "overdrive" 4¼ Litre model with its backward leaning mascot, always remember to turn the mascot sideways before you try to open the bonnet, otherwise you will be involved in a very sad incident.

In discussing long-distance touring, we cannot avoid the question of speed – both road speed and engine revolutions. It was precisely under these conditions – high speed touring on "motorways" – that problems with crankshafts first surfaced when the cars were new, and there is no reason to suppose that they have gone away in the intervening 70 years. The company's first action, it will be recalled, was to "red line" the revolution counter at 4500rpm, and today you must regard such a speed as an absolute maximum, not to be exceeded in any gear at any time. This is the point at which the main crankshaft vibration period sets in, and every slight reduction in revs below this level has a disproportionate effect in increasing the safety margin. It is generally accepted that if your engine never exceeds, say, 3800rpm and is maintained correctly it will go on almost for ever without a major failure.

This is all right as far as it goes, but it means that the owner of a standard 3½ Litre or 4¼ Litre model is limited to around 70-75mph. Although such a speed is acceptable for most people, there are those who want to travel a little faster on occasions, and for them the solution is to fit one of the overdrive conversions which are available, some of which have been developed specifically for the Derby Bentley. If you decide to go along this route, you must of course ensure that the remaining components of your car – brakes, steering and so on – are in tip-top condition, so that the car as a whole can deal with such speeds. Remember, too, that outside Germany the highest speed you can legally attain in most parts of the world is 80mph (130kph).

Whether you tour abroad or at home, or just attend club meetings, or merely use the car to go shopping, you can be sure that your Derby Bentley will fit in with the traffic, brighten the lives of those who watch it go by, and bring to yourself and your family many hours of innocent pleasure.

Chapter Ten

Ownership now

There will be some readers of this book who have yet to own a pre-war car, and others who have done so but who are unfamiliar with the Derby Bentley. In each case you will probably be asking yourself whether they are difficult beasts to own – are parts available, or is maintenance tricky? This chapter is aimed at reassuring you on both points.

The first, most often stated, and most often ignored advice is – join the relevant club first! If you intend to search for one of these delectable models, you can either do it on your own, and make the mistakes that many have made before you, or you can do it the easy way. Joining either the Bentley Drivers' Club or the Rolls-Royce Enthusiasts' Club – or ideally both – opens the door to help and expertise which you can draw on at every stage of the process. For a start, as we have mentioned previously, cars for sale are usually advertised in the club journals first, well before the owner takes the easy way out and places the car with a dealer. Quite apart from avoiding a dealer's margin in the transaction – which means a better price for both parties – most owners instinctively prefer to know that their car will go to another enthusiast rather than sit in an anonymous showroom. Secondly, whether you are intending to buy privately or from a trade source, the club experts can tell you the history of any car in great detail; remember that the Rolls-Royce and Bentley marques have probably the finest records of any make of car anywhere.

Thereafter, if you want specific help the two clubs are there to provide it. Between them they offer technical advice, spares, manuals, tools, training seminars, websites, specially tailored insurance schemes and many other services. Their regular magazines and advertising supplements are full of sensible articles on every aspect of ownership, not to mention advertisements from all the specialist firms offering repairs and restoration. Even more useful in many ways are the programmes of meetings, national and regional, since it is through talking to other owners in this way that you will be able to swap experiences and gain reassurance. Both have permanent headquarters buildings where staff are available to answer your queries throughout the week.

Quite apart from the two clubs, there are a wealth of commercial firms offering support. The question most prospective owners want answered is whether spares are easily available, and the answer is a resounding "yes". To begin with, there are still official Rolls-Royce spares available for Derby Bentleys, and the sole distributorship for these items is the famous London dealership of Jack Barclay. If this source cannot supply the part you want, then the next step is to try one of the specialist repair and restoration firms. There are many of these, and you will soon work out which are the major ones by watching the advertisements in the club journals, but probably the leading firm as far as Derby Bentleys are concerned are Fiennes Engineering of Little Clanfield, Oxford. They remanufacture numerous spares for these cars and will send a list on request. As well as a large number of engine and chassis parts – including valves, timing gears and even new cylinder heads (made from aluminium) – the firm are moving into the manufacture of body fittings such as lock and window winder mechanisms.

If the part you are seeking is still not obtainable, then it is possible that the Derby Technical Scheme within the Bentley Drivers Club can help. Participation in this scheme is by annual subscription, which brings you access not only to parts but also to expert technical advice. Pre-purchase car inspections and hire of workshop tools are also available under the Scheme. Secondhand parts are often available through the BDC, and this can be a godsend for rare, non-mechanical parts such as coachwork fittings. Remember too that, unlike the contemporary Rolls-Royce models, the Bentley uses a number of proprietary parts which are looked after these days by their relevant specialists. This would apply, for example, to SU carburettors, SU petrol pumps, horns, certain of the instruments (eg ammeter and petrol gauge), the Bijur chassis lubrication system and the Marles steering box (on later models).

As to how much maintenance you want to do on the car, and how much you would prefer to leave to a specialist firm, this is something which only you can decide and which depends on your temperament, your experience and the facilities you have available to you. It is no use even attempting an engine rebuild, for example, unless you have a hoist to remove the engine and a large bench where you can work on it. On the other hand there are a host of jobs which can be done on the engine without removing it, and which can be carried out in the most modest garage. What looks a difficult operation when you have never done it before will soon become routine if you are minded to persevere. The most important benefit in doing at least minor work yourself is that you become more familiar with the car's workings, and so you will be less likely to be defeated if some minor problem arises when you are on the road. Oil changes, for example, are within most people's capabilities, and the colour of the oil and the quantity of metal particles in the sludge will tell you much about the state of health of that component, be it engine, gearbox or rear axle.

Oil changes are something which can hardly be done too often. With the comparatively small mileage which most of us cover in these cars, it is unrealistic to carry out such a task on the basis of distance covered. At minimum you should change the oils once per year, and – as we have noted previously – this frequency should be greatly increased if you have had any major work carried out on the engine, at least until you are confident that all the old sludge has been removed. If your engine has been overhauled recently, or you know that it has been used and maintained regularly, then you can use a modern multigrade oil with confidence. Synthetic oils are probably not worth the considerable extra expense, as they have been developed specifically for the arduous conditions one finds in modern high-revving engines, and they will bring no additional benefit to a slow-speed, low-compression 1930s engine.

In spite of the so-called "one-shot" chassis lubrication system, there are a great many lubrication and other jobs which have to be carried out on a regular basis, and these are set out in great detail in the owner's handbook. If you were lucky enough to inherit a handbook with the car, so well and good. Otherwise, you will either have to pay a large sum for one from a secondhand book dealer, or you can spend rather less and buy a facsimile from the Club. One way or another it is worth getting hold of this superbly produced guide, as it will teach you a great deal, not only about routine maintenance but also about all the inner workings of your car. The manual will show you, for example, how to adjust the brakes and at what tension to set the fan belt. Tappet adjustment is also explained – a slightly more complicated task on this engine than on some others, since while

Brake adjustment is made easy with wing-nuts at each wheel.

measurement takes place as normal at the rockers the actual adjustment is done at the bottom of the pushrod rather than at the top. There is of course a circuit diagram, necessary when there are no less than nine fuses to check when there is a problem. Eight of these are rewirable rather than the cartridge variety, and the company thoughtfully provides a holder for a reel of fuse wire.

As to the "one-shot" system itself, we have agreed that it will pay you to check that this is in full working order, and if not to put it back to that state. Nowhere is that more important than in the feeds to the springs, where – as we learned earlier – the system is designed to deliver oil between the leaves so as to minimise any friction, and therefore damping action, between them. Getting the four springs to work properly in this way can transform the car's ride, from being rough and uncomfortable to a true "magic carpet" experience. Once these and all other areas of the one-shot system have been restored to full health, all you have to do thereafter is to keep the scuttle reservoir topped up and then press the operating pedal once every 100 miles.

Naturally if you intend to restore your car rather than merely maintain it then there are many firms who are ready to help you. Whether it is mechanical or body restoration you have in mind, you will want to compile some sort of shortlist of firms, based on what you can find out about them and in particular on recommendations from other owners who have actually used them. In this field as in many others, the rule that you get what you pay for certainly applies. As far as mechanical restoration goes, the Bentley specialists will aim to provide you with a standard of engineering equal to that of Derby in the 1930s. The other side of that coin, however, is that it will be just as expensive, in today's terms, as it was then – maybe more so, since the cost of skilled manpower has increased at very much more than the rate of inflation. Conversely you can often obtain good repair work at much lower prices, but it may well, for example, involve the use of off-the-shelf components, modified as necessary, instead of the real thing.

Where bodywork is concerned it is not necessary to use a Bentley or Rolls-Royce specialist, although if you do you can again rest secure in the knowledge that everything will be done to the highest standards. The fact is, however, that there are a great many firms or individuals offering coachbuilding skills, and this is an area where it can pay to shop around. If it is, say, merely an item of trim you want replacing, then a one-man firm in a back street may be able to do the job quite inex-

Tappet clearances are measured at the valve stem, while any adjustment is made lower down inside the valve chest.

The electrical circuits are well provided with fuses, of the rewirable variety

pensively – similarly for welding or spraying. If you are going to indulge in a major restoration, then it is important to set some ground rules. Given that a firm quote will probably not be possible, there should be at least an estimate, and preferably this should be broken down into estimated hours and an hourly rate so that it is easier to check invoices when they are submitted. You should also decide how much money you are prepared to commit, say, each month, and make it clear that the firm is to seek your consent before exceeding that amount. Remember to ask them to keep a photographic record – you will be glad of it in years to come if you decide to sell the car.

To summarise, then, you should have no qualms about being able to put your newly-acquired Bentley into a roadworthy state and to keep it so thereafter. Whether you elect to restore the car totally to concours condition, or alternatively to make it safe and reliable but no more, will be very much a personal choice based on budgetary considerations amongst others. Whatever you decide, however, you will have joined the ranks of thinking motorists who take pleasure in preserving our motoring history, and in demonstrating to the general public that 1930s-style motoring need not be too different from that of today.

Appendices

Appendix I: Show Cars

Chassis	Reg. no	Stand/Coachbuilder	Style	Finish	Price
1933					
B5AE	AUW101	Bentley Motors/ Vanden Plas	2d sports tourer	Ivory	£1380
B9AE	AND498	Bentley Motors/ Park Ward	4d 4l sports saloon	Pale blue	£1460
B17AE	AUU17	Bentley Motors/ Park Ward	Drophead coupé	Black	£1485
B19AE	US3474	Hooper	4d 4l sports saloon	Black/green	£1560
B21AE	ALX647	Barker	3-position dhc	Red	
B23AE	AUL1	Park Ward	2d sports saloon		£1635
B25AE	VH5750	Rippon	4d 4l sports saloon	Light blue	
B27AE	AXA444	Arthur Mulliner	4d 4l sports saloon	White/green	
B29AE	AUL31	Thrupp & Maberly	3-position dhc	Grey/red	£1495
B31AE	GS4254	H J Mulliner Owen	sedanca coupé	Grey/grey	£1550
1934					
B171BL	BBH360	Wm Arnold	Airflow saloon	Marina blue	
B183BL	BGU868	Arthur Mulliner	4d 4l sports saloon	Light blue/silver	
B2BN		Hooper	4d 4l sports saloon	Silver grey/blue	£1650
B4BN	BLB660	Gurney Nutting	2d 4l pillarless saloon coupé	Maroon	
B12BN		Rippon	4d 4l sports saloon	Grey/light blue	
B19BN	BLE672	Barker	Coupé de ville		
B22BN	BLR795	H J Mulliner	Concealed head dhc	Metallic rose	£1700
B30BN	BLA421	Thrupp & Maberly	4d 4l "aero-dynamic" saloon	Grey	£1695
B36BN	BLU131	Bentley Motors/Park Ward	Drophead coupé	Metallic two-tone blue	£1494
B46BN	JF7196	Bentley Motors/	Vanden Plas 2d tourer	Red/ivory	£1380
B50BN	BLB788	Bentley Motors/Park Ward	4d 4l sports saloon	Green	£1469
B60BN	BLC777	James Young	Drophead coupé	Blue/black	£1595
B64BN	EY5006	Cockshoot	4d 4l sports saloon	Black	£1575
B68BN	BLA217	Vanden Plas	4d 4l sports saloon	Silver/black	
B77BN	BTW158	Mann Egerton	4d 4l sports saloon	Platinum grey	£1600
B80BN	JU5763	Freestone & Webb	4d 4l sports saloon	Two-tone blue/grey	
B82BN	AWR166	Park Ward	4d 4l "streamline" saloon	Coronet red	£1848
1935					
B77EJ	DLW641	Windovers	2d 4l sports coupé	Yellow/black	
B105EJ	CGH648	Bentley Motors/ H J Mulliner	4d 4l sports saloon	Metallic two-tone blue	£1698
B107EJ	CLM971	Bentley Motors/ Vanden Plas	2d sports tourer	White	£1390
B111EJ	CJJ407	Bentley Motors/ Park Ward	Drophead coupé	Black	£1505
B123EJ		Wm Arnold	4d 4l "Slipstream" saloon	Birch grey	
B125EJ	CLA142	Freestone & Webb	4d 4l Brougham saloon	Birch grey	
B127EJ	CGX601	Hooper	2s 2l coupé cabriolet	Cream	£1730
B129EJ	BUE922	Rippon	2d 4l pillarless saloon	Silver grey	
B131EJ		Cockshoot	4d 4l sports saloon	Brown/fawn	
B133EJ	BYW318	Barker	2d 4l swept tail saloon	Green/green	
B135EJ	CGU170	Park Ward	2d 4l coupé de ville	Grey/grey	
B139EJ	CGW429	Gurney Nutting	2d 4l pillarless coupé	Metallic snow-shadow	
B141EJ	CLU74	H J Mulliner	4d 4l sports saloon	Two-tone metallic blue	£1680
B143EJ	CXA30	James Young	Drophead coupé	Metallic silver grey	£1595
B145EJ	CLC483	Vanden Plas	4d 4l pillarless saloon	Green	
B151EJ	VG8512	Mann Egerton	4d 4l sports saloon	Metallic silver-blue	£1596
B153EJ	BYP10	Arthur Mulliner	4d 4l sports saloon	Red/cream	
B155EJ	CGP888	Thrupp & Maberly	4d 4l "aerodynamic" saloon	Metallic grey	£1850
B195EJ	UN9028	Bentley Motors/Park Ward	4d 4l sports saloon	Green	£1480

Chassis	Reg. no	Stand/Coachbuilder	Style	Finish	Price
1936					
B157FC	DNU272	Bentley Motors/Park Ward	4d 4l sports saloon	Green	£1479
B88HK		H J Mulliner	4d 4l pillarless saloon	Black	
B92HK	DLD136	Arthur Mulliner	4d 4l sports saloon	Coronation red	
B110HK	DGT1	Bentley Motors/ Park Ward	4d 4l sports saloon	Grey	£1529
B112HK	DGW575	Bentley Motors/ Park Ward	Drophead coupé	Maroon	£1554
B114HK	DGW963	Bentley Motors/ Vanden Plas	2d sports tourer	Ivory/cream	£1440
B116HK	DNC567	Wm Arnold	4d 4l Slipstream saloon	Birch grey	
B118HK	DXN401	Gurney Nutting	4d 6l Airflow saloon	Steel dust	
B122HK	DGW967	Thrupp & Maberly	4d touring saloon	Cobalt violet	
B124HK	DTU726	Cockshoot	4d 4l sports saloon	Primrose/black	
B126HK	DXF992	James Young	Drophead coupé	Ivory	£1720
B128HK	VH9825	Rippon	4d 4l sports saloon	Silver grey	
B130HK	ELW43	Mann Egerton	4d 4l sports saloon	Metallic smoke blue	£1659
B132HK	DLF734	Barker	Fixed-head coupé	Yellow	
B136HK	YY1392	Freestone & Webb	4d 4l Brougham saloon	Duck egg green/ black	
B142HK	AXL1	Hooper	4d 4l saloon with division	Black	
B146HK	CWE940	Park Ward	Close-coupled all-steel saloon	Grey/maroon	£1700
B3HM	DLD273	Vanden Plas	4d all-weather	Dark green	
1937					
B77KU	EYT192	Carlton	4d 4l pillarless sports saloon		
B79KU	CVB702	H J Mulliner	Disappearing head dhc	Black	
B81KU	AVH300	Rippon	4d 4l sports saloon	Ivory	
B83KU	FLG659	Cockshoot	4d 4l sports saloon	Green/grey	
B85KU		Wm Arnold	4d 4l Slipstream saloon	White/ black mouldings	
B87KU	DOM277	Thrupp & Maberly	4d 4l touring saloon	Silver pearl	
B99KU	DFY177	Bentley Motors/ H J Mulliner	2d 4l High Vision saloon	Pastel green	£1814
B101KU	EXP74	Bentley Motors/ Park Ward	4d 4l sports saloon	White	£1529
B103KU	CNG555	Bentley Motors/Vanden Plas	Drophead coupé	Pale blue	£1549
B107KU		Bentley Motors/VandenPlas	2d special tourer	Light/dark grey	£1435
B111KU	ELR499	Park Ward	Pillarless saloon	Blue/white	£1825
B115KU	ELO3	James Young	Drophead coupé	Blue/ silver	
B117KU	CJW10	Mann Egerton	4d 4l sports saloon	Blue	
B119KU	EXX99	Gurney Nutting	4d 4l sports saloon	Graphite	
B121KU	ELD987	Windovers	Drophead coupé	Almond/ dawn grey	
B125KU	DLO555	Barker	4d 4l sports saloon	Blue	
B127KU	ELH565	Hooper	2d pillarless saloon coupé	Grey	£1845
B129KU	BYG176	Arthur Mulliner	4d 4l sports saloon	Silver grey	
B131KU	EGO709	Freestone & Webb	4d 4l Brougham saloon	Duck egg green/ black	
B133KU	FUG600	Vanden Plas	4d all-weather	Green	
1938					
B14MR	FWB653	Bentley Motors/ Park Ward	4d 4l sports saloon	Metallic nutria	£1624
B16MR	EYX399	Bentley Motors/ Park Ward	2d 4l special drophead coupé	Black	£1805
B18MR	EYX398	Bentley Motors/ H J Mulliner	4d 6l High Vision saloon	Beige/black	£1915
B20MR	EOM560	Bentley Motors/ Vanden Plas	2d sports tourer	Light red	£1520
B22MR	DKW287	Rippon	4d 6l saloon	Apple green	
B24MR	FND537	Wm Arnold	4d 4l Slipstream saloon	Marina blue	
B26MR		Hooper	2d coupé cabriolet	Red	
B28MR	FGT867	H J Mulliner	4d 4l High Vision saloon	Steel grey	
B30MR	FLU663	Park Ward	Fixed head coupé	Maroon	£1800
B32MR	FLE68	Thrupp & Maberly	4d 4l touring saloon	Green	£1820
B34MR		Cockshoot	4d 4l sports saloon	Cream	
B38MR	FGW386	James Young	Coupé de ville	Black/ bronze-beige metallic	
B40MR	FLH4	Gurney Nutting	Sedanca coupé	Black/cream	
B42MR	FLM21	Vanden Plas	2d 4l cabriolet	Metallic brown/gold	
B44MR	GCC1	Carlton	Drophead coupé, 2 str + dickey		
B46MR	FXP400	Mann Egerton	4d 4l sports saloon	Metallic dark grey	
B48MR		Freestone & Webb	4d 4l Brougham saloon	Maroon/black	

Appendix II: Road Test Data

Type	Year	Model	Price £	Weight as tested cwt	Braking at 30mph feet	Acceleration 0-30 secs	0-50 secs	0-60 secs	0-70 secs	Top max mph	Top mean mph	Mpg	Source
3½-Litre	1933	VdP tourer	1380	28.5						90			*Autocar* 6 Oct 1933
3½-Litre	1933	VdP tourer	1380	29.5	19*			18		91		16-18	*Motor* 7 Nov 1933
3½-Litre	1933	VdP tourer	1380	29	57**					91			*Motor Sport* Nov 1933
3½-Litre	1934	PW saloon	1460	30	31		13.4	20.4		91.8		16-18	*Autocar* 18 May 1934
3½-Litre	1935	PW dhc	1485	32.5	36		12.8			90		17-19	*Motor* 10 Dec 1935
4¼-Litre	1936	PW saloon	1510	33.5	36		10.6	14.8		96		17-19	*Motor* 21 Apr 1936
4¼-Litre	1936	PW saloon	1510	33.4	30		10.3	15.5	21.1	94.7	90.9	17	*Autocar* 8 May 1936
4¼-Litre	1936	PW saloon	1510	33	57**					93		13	*Motor Sport* Jun 1936
4¼-Litre	1937	PW saloon	1510	33.5	40		10.8			93.8	92.8	16.5	*Motor* 29 Jun 1937
4¼-Litre	1937	PW saloon	1510	34.4	30		12.7	17.1	24.2	91.8	88.0	16-17.5	*Autocar* 12 Nov 1937
4¼ (OD)	1939	PW saloon	1510	35.2	32		11.5	16.1	23.5	92.8	90.7	16-18	*Autocar* 7 Apr 1939
4¼ (OD)	1939	VdP dhc	1535	35.2	36	5.4	11.6	15.6	21.4	93?	89		*Motor* 2/23 May 1939

*from 20 mph **from 40 mph

Coachwork: VdP = Vanden Plas
PW = Park Ward
dhc = drophead coupé

Appendix III: Competitors – Road Test Data

Make	Year	Model	Price £	Weight as tested cwt	Braking at 30mph feet	Acceleration 0-50 secs	0-60 secs	0-70 secs	Top max mph	Top mean mph	Mpg	Source
Alvis	1932	Speed 20 tourer	695	26	25				89	89	18	*Autocar* 13 May 1932
Talbot	1933	105 saloon	795	35	30	14.6	19.4			88	16	*Autocar* 23 June 1933
Lagonda	1933	M45 tourer	795	32.5			14.2		92		16	*Motor* 14 Nov 1933
Alvis	1936	3½-litre saloon	1270	38	33	12	17		93	93	17	*Motor* 4 Feb 1936
Railton	1936	Eight saloon	628	24	26	8.6	11.5	16	91.8		15-17	*Autocar* 21 Feb 1936
Talbot	1936	3½-litre saloon	825	35.6	31	11.8	16.8	24	92.8	89.1	15	*Autocar* 3 Apr 1936
Lagonda	1938	V12 saloon	1550	39.6	32.5	9.7	12.9	17.9	103.4	100.3	12-15	*Autocar* 11 Mar 1938
Alvis	1938	Speed 25 saloon	885	39	30.5	11.1	15.0	21.9	96.8	95	17-18	*Autocar* 10 Jun 1938
Lagonda	1938	LG6 saloon	1195	38.7	33	11.3	16.4	23.0	95.7	91.4	12-14	*Autocar* 17 Jun 1938
SS Jaguar	1939	3½-litre saloon	445	32.9	31.5	9.8	14.4	19.8	90.9	88.2	16-18	*Autocar* 28 Apr 1939
Alvis	1939	4.3 saloon	995	40	35.5	9.5	13.1	18.0	100	96.5	16-17	*Autocar* 2 Jun 1939